Young: And Having Faith N the Hood

SOULJA SOULJA

Rodney L. Clark Jr.

DEDICATION

This guidebook is dedicated first and foremost to my beautiful, never-forgotten deceased daughter; Dymond. Your dad won't stop at nothing to make you as happy as I would if you were still living. Also, I dedicate this to my children Dymani and Dyshawn(Bear).

About This Book

I created this book because I felt the need to reach out to the young adults and the youth and try my best to guide them on just about all of the obstacles that we face while growing in the hood. We really need positive minded people to step in and intervene on some of the crisis and challenges that we are facing every day. There are far too many people that are jumping on the bandwagons and mimicking and imitating what other lost, misguided people are doing and we are losing our 'kings' and 'queens' rapidly to foolish thinking and foolish acts.

The contents in this book are very similar to how I create 'RapSpire' music. The messages are the same, and the end goal is the same. I want to see us do better as people. I want to see us do better as adults. I want to see us do better by our children. My stomach turns as I hear and see a lot of the ignorance that goes on nowadays. My heart pours out as I see the damage that we are creating within one another. I think about the women that are being destroyed by the men. I think about the men that are being destroyed by the women. I think about the innocent kids that are being caught up in the crossfire.

In this book I felt the need to get real with my people about drugs/alcohol, partying, gangs, drug dealing, jail, prison, men/women/children, and immorality. As well as politics, success, goals, jobs, skills, and parenting. We can use a lot of help in these areas. I have noticed too many of us, including myself, that feel like we got these areas all figured out; when we really don't. We are destroying ourselves. We are destroying the men, women, and children all together; and at the same time. We are trying to get all of the attention and striving to look rich, but the reality is that we are struggling and broke. We have to quit pretending and faking for each other and accept the fact that we have some serious work to do.

But, we aren't all bad people. We are actually very intelligent. We are able to support one another. We are able to love one another. We are able to uplift one another. We have to get out of this mindset that it is a race though. We have to realize that we are unique individuals that will get so much further if we learn to stick together. This book isn't to downgrade us, but it is to realistically point out the areas that we need to give some deep thought to, and to stop dismissing the problems; or just simply passing them off.. This book acknowledges a bunch of problems, but it also draws up the solutions too.

I want the reader to know that no matter what, I come from the hood too. I still live in the hood and have the same hood mentality, so I know what I'm talking about for real.

CONTENTS

ACKNOWLEDGMENTS

Special thanks to Kenneth Gunn for being the reason that I even decided to turn this manuscript into a book, and his support for the content. Special thanks to my family and to my friends that have supported everything that I do with my ambitious mind; especially my father Rodney Sr., who encourages me and supports anything that I do without turning a deaf ear or a blind eye to none of my many ventures. I won't stop at nothing to be successful as well as become an inspiration and a role model for the youth and the young adults. I dedicate this to every young teenager and every young adult that is dedicated to becoming somebody even though we all come from the hood. I put this together for US! This is for YOU.

Mama's Bad Child

Imagine mama's precious little baby that didn't have a care in the world. The innocence that covered your face. The smile that began her morning. Her reason for being alive. The reason she bragged. The first reason she knew true love. The baby that taught her how to become a woman. To walk as a responsible lady. Can you imagine how she thought of your future? How she did anything to keep you safe and protected? Although you will never remember, think about how she sacrificed her life to keep you fed, sheltered, and loved. Think about the emotions she experienced watching you grow before her eyes. Think about the pain she felt every time she heard you cry. Think about it! Then ask yourself how you were the reason she smiled, then grew to be mama's bad child?

Out of four children, I was the oldest, and the coldest. The curious one. The rebellious one. The one who could hear well, but only listened to what I wanted to listen to. It always seems to be one in every household. A complaining, no bills paying, gotta have it my way, egotistical hard-headed child. Mama's bad child. The one that jumped off the porch around thirteen or fourteen years old. The one that had no regards for the law, so they made it easier for themselves to get into trouble. Then they wound up having to call on mama. Acting a fool in school; the school came down on mama. Fell off into drugs/alcohol, now you acting out on mama. Always have the desire to, but know you can't take care of yourself, but you still wanna trip on mama.

Now mama recognizes game on the changes in her once so innocent, once so precious child, that she begins to lash out on her child.

1

SOULJA SOULJA

Something she never wanted, nor desired to ever have to do. And since her child is aggressive, under the influence, and sensing anger; decides to snap back and lash out even more rebelliously. Forcing mama to lose trust, take away privileges, and sometimes alienate her poisoned child that doesn't recognize that they are the problem; and the solution. This child doesn't hear nor care about the tears mama cries in the middle of the night. I was once this child.

I could make up excuses as to why I acted out and blame things on my upbringing or things that I'd witnessed in my youth. I could not recognize mama for how she was raised and try not to take in mind that she raised me the best way she could; considering the drama and/or turmoil she may have experienced in her life before and after me. I could blame it on what I felt like I didn't have and try to make her feel like less of a parent, without knowing the struggles I would face as an adult/parent, or how my own children would be raised. I could simply just say that I wasn't happy with the way that I was raised, without acknowledging that I was always fed, clothed, sheltered, loved, supported, schooled, and happy before I created my own unhappiness.

But with what she had to offer mama did the best that she could do. She provided for me and my siblings. And even into adulthood she still does. Luckily for her, I was ungrateful enough to make the rest of my siblings never want to put her through the same occurrences. And they didn't either. As an adult, I am embarrassed and saddened by the way that I treated my mother. And I pay for it by being as old as I am and still not where I should be in life. I have younger siblings that don't look up to me and wouldn't dare want to be like me. They prospered faster than me as well. I still bump my head with bad habits that I developed back in my rebellious youth that keep on pulling me down further. Constantly fighting the law and getting further caught up in the system is my main problem. The same type of peers that have always dragged me further down I still can't shake. There is a list of things that resulted from disrespecting and becoming mama's proud, bad child. Worst of all, I live every day hearing her voice telling me to stop drinking, smoking, hanging with bad crowds, getting into trouble; all of the things that would destroy me later on in life. But I didn't listen. I wasn't going to listen. Now I'm stuck wishing that I could stop smoking, drinking, gang banging, and getting into trouble. I wish that I had a wife that loved me and I loved her. I wish that I could get ahead in life. But I'm stranded right where I am because I created debt that I have to pay for well into adulthood. And my first mistake of all was becoming mama's bad child. And to think kids/teens think that they are exempt from the consequences of their actions that they currently make. Nope they follow you right into adulthood. Especially when you know better.

Honoring Your Parents

When I was a young child, I acknowledged the presence of my parents. When I was a teen, I resisted my parents. As an adult, I respect and honor my parents. But I wish that I would have had this same level of respect and honor all along. Sadly, it took me to become a mature adult to realize the importance of their love, and leadership, and presence. The young mind is fully capable of honoring their parents the way they should be honored though.

Although we can't all say that we lived like the *'Cosby's,'* we still must acknowledge the love, sacrifices, and dedication. Our parents weren't designed to be perfect, but they were designed for us and we are reflections of them. The adopted and fostered children even found their ways into loving homes that God made for them as part of His plan. Our parents are our first mentors, first teachers, our first loves, and our first providers. Before you knew who you were, or where you were you were already being loved, held, rocked, fed, sheltered, trained, and raised. This is all before you found your individual, unique personality. Before you gained your independence. Before you cared about how you looked. Before you faced any of the challenges of life on your own. Parents were there every morning to keep you from being scared. To keep you protected from the evils and dangers. To answer all of your questions about life. If yours did these things and you know it, no amount of wrongdoing on their part could justify why you couldn't honor them forever for these things alone.

Understand something, every parent was once a child before. They too had parents, siblings, uncles, aunts, and cousins. They had grandparents. They had their own immediate family that bought them up and raised them however it was that they did. They had their own things, whether good or bad, that they had to witness and endure. They had pressures as well. These ways, environments, and living conditions shaped who they are as a person just the same as yours did for you. The ways they react to things and the ways that they think mostly stem from how they were raised. The same with you. If they didn't think something was right in their upbringing, they most likely learned the right way and changed. This explains how you were raised slightly different in ways. Most parents carry similar attitudes, characteristics, and thinking as their immediate family though. The same thing you will tend to do. This doesn't make them abnormal or undeserving of honor and respect just because you don't agree. Heredity and genetics plays very important roles in how we think and act. You have free will to change how you think and act, as you will feel similar to them, but this is what will make you unique but not *better than* though. Mothers and fathers receive a bad rap at times by their children simply because children don't understand this. They also haven't experienced how their own children will respond to the things that they do, say, think, and react. They haven't experienced how much they will find out that they are much like their own parents. Parenting didn't come with any guidebooks so parents do what they feel is right. What makes them imperfect is what they do that they know is wrong. Even still, that is their problem that they will have to deal with. As long as you know that you are fed, sheltered, and clothed God will deal with their imperfections. Don't condemn your parents for their ways and thinking without first examining who raised them, around what, and how. If they had a rough upbringing they will naturally reflect that, and in turn have a rougher time raising their own children. If it was all good, they usually do better. Be considerate. This goes for fathers too. They may not have done what they were supposed to, but if you learned anything from them, honor them still. In some kind of way, you are still a reflection of them. Not honoring your parents doesn't change them, nor will it ever make your life easier or better. Dishonoring them will only draw the parent and child relationship further apart and make matters worse. It does nothing but make you miss out on valuable training and life lessons you can learn from them. You don't fully learn who you are as a person. Meaning, you don't fully understand why you look, think, act, and feel the ways that you do. Even parents that didn't do their best realize the least that they could do is to help you learn who you are and teach you what they can about life. They always can help you in some kind of way no matter whom they are or what kind of lifestyle they live or lived. Honor your parents, because even as an adult you will find that you need them about just as much as you did when you were a child. And for much larger situations too.

Why The Same People/Same Situations

I've wondered lots of times why I can't seem to move ahead in life? Why do I keep attracting the same people? Why do I keep repeating the same situations? Why do I have the brightest ideas but can't seem to execute them and make them successful?

I've come to the conclusion that I have never changed the person that I am. I can honestly tell myself that besides the houses, cars, and the kids I am pretty much doing the same things that I was doing as a teenager. Of course with time you become more knowledgeable and should naturally become more mature, but other than that, nothing much has changed. The same crowds that I attracted and was attracted to is still the same. I still have the same drug and alcohol habits; maybe even worse. This includes experimenting with other drugs as well. I have similar thoughts. I like the same type of women/girls. I still have very little regard for the law. I still talk the same.

This explains why I am still affiliated with the same gang members; plus met and accompanied more over the years. This is why I still have a *gangsta* mentality. This explains why my criminal record is filled with drug and alcohol related convictions. This explains why I still can get pulled over and at any time cops can find drugs in my car or smell alcohol on my breath. This leads to my arrest and conviction. It explains why over and over I am paying out more and more money to the county for legal fees, substance abuse classes, and court ordered programs. This is an example of taking from your own

7

household and just giving away the hard earned money. This explains why the ladies in my life are just as hopeless and strung out as me. This is why I've never had a real woman. It explains why I don't even attract real women. I am still turned on and tempted by the slutty types. By the one night stands. By the easy ones. By the adventure seekers. By the *wild child* girls with nothing going for themselves. I attract the girls that are surrounded by multiple children that they can't even take care of, with multiple '*baby daddies.*'

This explains why I find it easy to drink and drive, to carry pistols, to drive without a license, to sell drugs, and to catch case after case. I have no regard for the law and always will try to find ways to outsmart the system, or get around the laws. This explains why I still curse with every phrase that I use. It explains why I still speak disrespectfully while easily and naturally referring to women as bitches and hoes. This is why my tongue is so sharp and I say whatever I feel like saying no matter who it hurts.

Just when I thought I was grown and mature I realized that I hadn't grown up at all. I still carry the same characteristics that I developed with my earlier underdeveloped, unskilled mind. This is why I keep landing in the same situations. This is why those around me haven't changed. I haven't changed. And until I do, things will stay the same around me. Because I've seen people in every age level, well into their sixties, that are sitting in jails or have completely jacked up lives. So that tells me right there that there is really no age limit on stupidity and keeping the same life patterns going.

Drug Abuse/Alcoholism/Partying

Oh my how the eighties and nineties babies are extremely obsessed with abusing drugs, alcohol, and partying. I, myself, have had these same obsessions since I was fifteen years old. Fifteen years later, I've seen a generation of zombies that barely have anything going for themselves except being smoked out, out of shape bodies. Aged faces. Too many kids. Too little success stories.

On any given weekend you could easily witness somebody you know on the way to the club or the bar that has to have a pack of cigarettes, a bottle of liquor, a bag of weed, a pack of blunts, a party pack of ecstasy pills, a new outfit, and a fresh pair of shoes. And they need all of this upon arrival. One night of fun could easily run up a two to three hundred dollar tab if you include admission fees, bar money, and munchies at the end of the night. It is unbelievable how all of these things have become a priority, and you have some addicts who live to do this three, four, or five times out of every week.

The result from all of this is going to be a complete shutdown of the body by the time they reach their forties and fifties. And they don't even know it. Drunken girls are leaving with big, bad wolves; and going home with them and winding up with '*club babies*.' Their kids are constantly being passed from house to house to different babysitters. When they wake up in the morning they rush home to their kids with major hangovers and can barely tend to the children's needs. Worse than that, kids wake up and see mommy in the bed with different men/wolves all of the time.

SOULJA SOULJA

Our men are landing in jail on drug and alcohol related charges every time they turn around. They are so high and drunk at bars and clubs that they end up in unsuspecting dramas and fights. Sexually transmitted diseases (STD's) are passed around in great numbers because of drunken, unprotected sexual encounters. Men are forced to be *'baby daddies'* to women that they don't even care anything about. All of this focus on partying and substance abuse has people spending too much money and time on all the wrong things and winding up in all of the wrong places. On occasion, these types of nights can be fun. But people with nothing to do, no goals in place, neglecting the needs of their children, and not taking care of the home-front always seem to overindulge, excessively drink, keep themselves drugged, and can't stop partying.

People are taking in too much of these things and not understanding that these things done excessively will cause permanent harm to your body, your mental, and others around you. Drunken conversations start fights and cause people to give their word on things that they don't need to attempt to execute. Drugs and alcohol become so addictive that you won't even realize the excessive amounts that you are taking. Partying too much puts you at much higher risks of drunk driving, having drugs in the car, losing focus of what relationship you already have, and just meeting too many unnecessary people in general. There is a slight difference in those that do these things in moderation, but they too put themselves at risk of overindulging.

There is so much more important things to spend our time and money on. How can you love and focus on your man or woman when there are constantly *'little red riding hoods'* and *'big bad wolves'* jumping out at you? How can you chase a dream when everyday you are chasing a high? Who's going to take you seriously when they realize that you never even remember or know what you are saying or said because you are always drunk or high when you are social? We need a generation that consists of: more leaders, more entrepreneurs, more graduates, and business people that still enjoy life but are determined to make progress and changes. We don't need any more drug addicts and zombies gathering to do nothing but enjoy each others' drunk and high company. I mean if you don't have a plan, a goal, or are where you should be in life what exactly are you celebrating/partying so much for?

Ignorant Thinking Amongst Black Youth

Growing up in the hood, I was an initiator, and a victim of ignorant thinking and showcasing ignorant ways. Black youth have long become slaves to the ignorant minds coming up in ghettos and poverty ridden societies.

These days everybody is so pressured to be hard. Pressured to have the most money. Pressured to have the fanciest car. Pressured to look the best. But, there is very little pressure to be the most successful. Less pressure to have the best job. Less pressure to be the best parent. Less pressure to own your own piece of land. Less pressure to stay out of trouble.

It seems as if black youth are mostly caught up in the '*setup-to- fail*' mindset that the only way to make money is to work; and if I can't get hired, sell drugs. Selling drugs has been taking lives and breaking up black families and homes since drugs graced the scene; and stricter laws followed in the 1990's. When the only proven way out is death and/or prison, we still get caught up in the fast, easy money and put our families and ourselves at risk when we know and fully understand the outcome already. I've seen people hustle for years. Ten year strong runs. Then, they turn around and have a judge sentence them to double the amount of years of their run. No matter how much they've gained, they end up with nothing. But still, the *dopeboy* life is widely glamorized in the black society, and hugely popularized in rap music. It is time to wake up youngsters. No matter how many songs he says it in a successful rapper no longer, or may never have, sells or sold dope. It is merely entertainment, only popularized because the whole industry knows you are going to buy it, and buy into it. Neither do they really care if you die by it.

There are many ignorant ways of thinking that I could elaborate on. Every little thug wants to be the biggest gangster. These idiots live their entire life trying to prove to their friends that they can bang harder, shoot, kill, go to jail, do prison time more or better than the next one alike. All of the most ignorant activities you can achieve in life. They spend their lives talking about what they will do, who they have shot or killed, and how many times they've been to the joint. They poison the minds of the youngsters under them; while they spend their lives dodging and catching bullets, watching their backs, being forced to carry guns, spending more time imprisoned than free, and then eventually dead. What's so ignorant about this type of person is that they really think people admire them or care about what they do. This type of thug is usually broke, and whenever they get killed or wind up in prison for decades no one will even care.

Young black women feel their children don't need their fathers around at all. This is some or the dumbest, most ignorant thinking that I've ever thought I'd encounter. Black youth being obsessed with how many people they can sleep with is a shame as well. In fact, some live their day to day lives trying to get the next score. Grown men and women thinking that it's alright to get drunk, do drugs, party, show sexual immoralities, curse, fight, and fuss in front of our children is an outrage. Also, there are the parents that gangbang, and teach their children how to gangbang. Parents are just simply birthing children and watching them grow up without teaching them anything positive. And these are the ones that have multiple children. There is just so much ignorance out there. Everybody wants to look flamboyant but most are too broke to live the way that they appeal to others. Everybody is partying but a small percentage has goals for tomorrow, or even a job.

YOUNG: AND HAVING FAITH N THE HOOD

We have to realize that our ancestors suffered much for our
freedoms. Because you were born free doesn't mean you should
forget that we haven't been free for very long at all. We were slaves
for hundreds more years than we have actually been free. Our black
leaders were still fighting for our rights as black citizens well into the
1970's. We are spitting in their faces and stomping on all of their
hard works and accomplishments by displaying such ignorance. This
is not just a black thing, it's a human thing that involves all races. I
care about the way we act and our image in society. Good and
intelligent black people are tired of being stereotyped alongside
proud, ignorant, clueless black people. If these young, wild and free,
*we don't give a f**** attitudes keep up the way that they have been
this will be a destroyed race that will surely kill ourselves and
continue to kill each other in the process. It is enough of the hatred
toward each other as well. It is time to inspire and uplift each other
all over this country. No matter what culture or color. It is time to
reshape our black society. It is time to eliminate the ignorance that
has spread to our children that will also spread to their children. We
need to stop this cycle.

Why Stay Focused In School

Twelve years later, after graduation, one way that I really realized I played and lost an important game in life was at the point when I decided it was cool to not take school seriously. This, realizing it years later, was by far one of my ultimate mistakes. Sadly I can remember teachers, guidance counselors, my mother, and my girlfriend urging me to start being more serious about my education. Now I understand more than ever why it was important to stay focused in school.

Over and over I've repeated to myself and to other young people that if I could redo my attendance, behavior, and work ethic in school over again, I would do things so much differently. I would have never let drugs, gangs, and girls take over my mind and leave me unfocused on my important education. I would have never let status, rank, or reputation define me. I would have never tried to fit in or get caught up in how others influenced me. These ways include dressing, sex, ignorant thinking, and behaviors. I would have never let myself get caught up in drama.

Even sadder, I was an honor roll student all the way up until my high school years. I completely played myself by falling off into smoking marijuana after completing the eighth grade. Getting off into smoking marijuana, while still attending school, was by far the dumbest thing that I would live to regret from then to my late twenties; even more than dealing with girls. Drugs completely destroyed my willingness to be anything anymore. I recall telling teachers and counselors that I wasn't interested in attending college. I recall them responding to me in so many words by saying, "You are too smart to be so dumb." And I was. I knew how to keep my grades up in school. All you really had to do was do the work. I did the work in school only. Whatever needed to be taken home didn't get done. Stupid, stupid, stupid decision. I passed by doing only what I could do at school. No focus at all. My normal routine was to go to school, get off the bus after school and get high. I averaged smoking about six blunts a day with my drop out homeboys. I did keep a job in school, but girls and weed were the after school agenda. Go to school, leave and get high, go to work, come home and get on the phone, wake up and repeat the process was the routine. Never did I focus in high school and I had all the potential to do much better. I kept a C grade point average by simply doing the school work so I was able to graduate. Even with scholarships and programs that assisted me, I still had no desire to take advantage. Nor did I take the time to figure out what I really wanted to do with my life after graduating. I already had girls and I was already used to making money and working. Maybe I thought these things would carry me through life. Boy was I wrong and couldn't be dumber.

As I say, twelve years later and over the years, I found myself working way too many dead end jobs. Some could have become great careers, but I didn't learn how to focus at my first job; which was school. So in the real world, I didn't focus correctly at any other job. Switching jobs constantly kept me at minimum wage pay. This affected how I was able to maintain a household. I kept girls as a primary focus, so I suffered the pressures of love, lust, and heartache too soon to even know how to handle it. I made children early in life with someone that I was unsure of, and had nothing but problems out of her every since. I found myself taking care of a family I wasn't even stable enough or financially ready for. Another primary focus I had while I should've been paying attention in school was the drugs. Into adulthood, all of my friends have either been dealers or addicts. And I literally mean every last one of them. I have a criminal background full of drug charges. I can't seem to stop doing the drugs no matter how bad I want to. Only unless I landed on probation and was forced to stop. I am still involved with the same gang members. No one around me is a positive, educated person that can show me how to strive for better in my life. My actions have caused me to lose my mother's trust before I hit eighteen years old. I never knew how important having her trust was until I lost it. If I wasn't dedicated right now to getting my life on track and getting back into school, I could most likely classify myself as one of the losers. I would have much rather been considered a nerd in school, and actually turned out to be someone before the age thirty than to be still lost in life because I chose to be dumb and not stay focused in school when I had the chance. So when they tell you to stay in school and do your best and stay focused, take it from me, those are million dollar words. You should really consider listening to them.

Pick Up A Book—And Read

This digital age has provided us a number of outlets to reach out to the world and get information at a rapid pace. Most people who desire information turn to the internet. Although, the internet is a *Godsend* for receiving information on a particular subject quickly, it is still highly capable of providing too much cluttered information, or the wrong information. Nothing is better for researching than picking up an old fashioned book.

People get so wrapped up in seeing things on the Internet and hearing others quote what they've seen on the internet. The information is taken in so fast and attention is shifted to the next available piece of detail or information so fast that it makes the internet sort of an unreliable source for studying material.

Books aren't filled with ads off to the side, and a dozen different things you can click on and shift your attention to while you are trying to focus on what you came to see. If you wanted to study and learn more about Africa, for example, try typing in 'Africa' into a search engine. You would never get a more in depth teaching of 'Africa' on the internet, or any other subject, than you would at your local library. There is an old saying that, *"If you want to keep a person from learning something, put the information inside a book. They will never read it."* People nowadays want to process information fast. And using the internet, fast results is just what they get too. I find it interesting when people learn something really fast on the internet then broadcast it to everyone like they have it all figured out. They don't even know the half.

Reading a book is fundamental and always will be. No distractions. No deceptive articles to throw you off. Books are a great exercise for the mind, body, and soul. So open your mind a little more and receive so much more from a good ol' book.

Follow The Followers

Good leadership is growing nonexistent. The new leaders are actually the followers. So the new thing is to follow the followers. Instead of one brave person taking an intelligent brain and making other brains stronger and more knowledgeable, another person jumps off of a bandwagon and shares their brain with anyone that will follow. Sharing what they've stolen and added their own twist to, forcing you to think that they were smart enough to come up with what it is they're showing or telling.

The best scenario is Facebook. Look at how many bird-brained, recent nobodies have gained a group or bird-brained followers to feed them all of the poison that they've learned from somewhere else. I just get a kick out of every girl on Facebook making ugly duck lips all of a suddenly. I also have taken notice of how they all make the same poses in their pictures. When a celebrity says a catchy phrase, one follower acknowledges it, says it, now the whole following Facebook community must repost and repeat. They can clearly see everyone saying and doing the same thing, but it burns them up not to follow the trend. Now everybody speaks the same phrases in their conversations. There are artists and celebrities and companies just sitting back getting rich off of these poor souls.

These followers that are leading the followers are just as simple-minded as the people following them. They can post their minds freely behind a computer or cell phone, but when you try to have an intelligent conversation with them you lose them every time. Why? They can't communicate intelligently. They only know stupidity and following the latest trendy topics and phrases. The intelligent one will realize that they are talking to a brick wall. The follower will remain silent throughout because they can't comprehend since no one has intelligent conversations with them. When you school them it doesn't mean anything. They return back to their followers and bless them with more simple-minded garbage. This is why so many people have the same style. They think and speak the same way. They dress similarly. They look to see where everyone else is hanging out, and what they are doing, then they plan their lives around that. Who's really standing out and trying to do something different? Who's really creating a platform that others can be proud to be a part of? It looks to me like the majority is just following followers of things that don't really mean a thing, and stand for nothing.

Friends and Loyalty

It's a great feeling to have friends. But the older you get, the harder it is at welcoming new friends into your life. Love and loyalty is a must when choosing who you allow into your life, your situations, around your family, and with your heart. New people, filled with the new wickedness of the world, have taken loyalty and replaced it with ulterior motives, further making it harder to trust so called friends even more.

It seems that the more digital and social this world has become, the less likely it is for people to stick around. We are meeting more and more people, and allowing them in our lives just off of what we heard or think is true about them. Portraying them as such, while it is recognizable to them, gives them more ammo to fake to you about who they really are. The same is true the other way around. People think a certain way about you, based on what they think or heard; and want to be around you for those reasons. You notice ulterior motive when you see they're only around you for those obvious reasons that really have nothing to do with caring about your real person.

Someone may want to ride around with you every day because you have an attractive car; but they hate the music you listen to in that attractive car. The music you listen to identifies your character more than the car though. Someone may want to be around you because you naturally attract all the attention from the crowd they want to attract; but they hate when you are at home with your family. The family that you take care of identifies your true character more than the attention that you receive from particular people though. There is no loyalty amongst these type of peers that can only identify with you in the type of way that they want to, instead of what identifies your true person. The ones I really can't stand are the ones that love to be around you but they run when you have your children around. If you can't accept my children being around then you definitely can't accept me.

The 'day one' friends have mostly proved to be the most loyal friends. Not in all situations though. There have been numerous instances when 'day one' friends that you've befriended since early childhood have grown envious and displayed jealousy as adulthood kicked in. There are numerous instances when crime partners from 'day one' have turned into snitches when they were caught up. It has grown more and more difficult to trust any of your friends, past and present. The world and the people in it have become so evil in their ways that everyone seems to be looking out for only themselves. People are using whoever they can for whatever they can. They are scheming on each other. They are preying on each other. They are doing all of this while still smiling in the other person's face. Sexual immorality is so bad now that you never know which so-called friend is secretly plotting on your spouse.

I don't know of a time when you could trust everybody that you hang with. I do know that a true friend naturally, and by all means, wants to see the other person prosper in life. They tell them only what they know is right. They never scheme, they never plot. I personally believe there are too many people who have nothing going for themselves that are trying to befriend people who do have something going for themselves. I am a firm believer in people hanging with their own kind. If you know that you are lazy, hang with other lazy people. Don't come around the motivated and active and get mad because they have a job and productive things to do. If you are a playa, hang around other playas. Don't come around a married person and be mad because they are always spending time with their spouse. If you are simple-minded and think ignorantly, hang around other simple-minded, ignorant people. Don't come around smart people and be mad because they use logic and reasoning when thinking and making decisions. This will do nothing but anger you. It will cause you to be envious. It will cause that person to be confused. These types of encounters will never create a friendship, nor will it create a relationship that will last even a minute. If you've ever had somebody feel indifferent about you they would have given off signs that you can recognize quickly. It's the same thing when someone else notices you have an indifferent feeling about them. Although it is extremely difficult nowadays, only deal in healthy friendships where it is obvious the two, or group, has true loyalty and all parties best interest at heart. There should be no ulterior motives. You would be better off alone than to have a snake friend bite you in the end. Eventually, that is exactly what is going to happen.

What is a 'Real Nigga'

I must discuss a term that is widely used amongst black culture and highly expressed in rap music as the thing to be. This term is a '*real nigga*.' What exactly is a '*real nigga*?' Is it really a requirement these days to be a '*real nigga*' if you are an African American? The way the term is used you are nothing to black society if you are not a '*real nigga*.'

We all know what the word '*real*' means. So we should discuss the definition of the word '*nigga*.' '*Nigga*' is short/slang for the original term '*nigger*.' A '*nigger*' is a derogatory term that was used by white people during slavery to describe a black person. The dictionary definition for the word '*nigger*' is defined as, 'a member of a socially disadvantaged class of persons' or '*a black person*.' A black person who was not allowed to read, to write, or to get an education; therefore, an illiterate person was described as a '*nigger*.' Since then, black folks have adopted the term, shortened it, and refer to each other as a '*nigga*' or '*my nigga*'-which is a widely used term that can be heard mentioned by nearly all of the black youth. Now we have decided to pressure each other into being '*real niggas*.'

A '*real nigga*' is what more than 90% of the young, black males strive to be. Although, I believe everyone has a different, unique definition of what a '*real nigga*' is, or does. For most that claim to be a '*real nigga*,' it doesn't involve being anything positive, nor does it involve doing anything positive. When I think about the term and the people whom have adopted it into their lifestyle, I have to once again think about what the original '*nigger*' is. It is an illiterate, black person who can't read or write. It is a black person who is denied an education. Then, I think of all the young blacks today who can't read or write and hate to learn anything that would make them a positive person that is able to do good things for themselves or their families. I think about the twenty year old boy that I met in jail; who justifies being sentenced to twenty five years in prison for robbing a jewelry store saying, "*real niggaz* do real things." I think about all the black males in prisons or in jails saying that they are there and did what they did because they are '*real niggaz*.' I think of the people who say all the '*real niggaz*' are locked up. I think of all the '*real niggaz*' who are dead. I think about all the self proclaimed '*real niggaz*' that have no other skills except selling drugs. I guess there are a number of things '*real niggaz*' do, but most of it seems to fall in line with what an illiterate person who can't read, write, or learn would do.

So with that being said, the term '*real nigga*' seems to be correct in describing the person who claims to be such. But my question is, "Why would anyone want to be a '*real nigga*?" That sounds to me like they are calling themselves a '*real, illiterate black person*.' Wouldn't it make more sense to be a '*real African American*' or a '*real black person*?' Why would you degrade yourself? Terms are popularized so much today that people don't even bother to stop and think about what they are saying or claiming into their lives. What do you call a black person that stays out of jail, works a job, and takes good care of their families? What do you call black males that go to college and further their education? What do you call black leaders that make a difference in society? What about the ones that hopes to bring out positivity in themselves and others? That's the type of person I'd rather be. If '*real niggaz*' have to stay in and out of jails, deal drugs, have no real skills, not take care of their children, kill each other, and constantly watch their backs; I'd rather just be a '*real black man*.' Don't compare me to an illiterate person on any day. Definitely don't compare me to a proud, illiterate person at that. I've learned too much and come too far to be classified as such. We all have, and if not, we've all had the opportunity to. Even if black men who make an effort to grow wiser and be somebody positive and do good in their life are classified as '*soft*' or whatever, I'll gladly take that classification over being lacking, imprisoned, and/or illiterate. But if the term fits you, wear it. I am not one to judge. I just find it hard to stomach how young blacks can lower their values and do and say senseless things that have proven to ruin the lives of so many of us. All of this for a lifestyle and a title that is glamorized, but yet so degrading.

Young Black People and their Obsession with Fashion

I once noticed a young, twenty something year old white couple in a waiting room at a doctor's office. They were holding each other, and casually talking back and forth while waiting on the doctor. I couldn't help but notice how happy they looked together, and I figured that they were in love. I mean, you normally don't see a young man attending a doctor's appointment with his girlfriend. As they sat across from me, I glanced down and noticed both of them had on dirty shoes. I'm talking about old and dirty shoes on their feet. They both had them. Their threads weren't that hot as well. They seemed to have just thrown on anything and rushed out into public.

I now caught myself paying close attention to the attire that this couple was wearing more than I paid attention to the affection that they displayed for each other. I then thought to myself about how black people have an unusual obsession with fashion and looking good. And besides the couple of dust busters that you see hanging around in their own zones, I thought about how I never really have seen young black people dressing down and dirty. They definitely weren't going to approach the public wearing dirty shoes.

Black youth will wear a pair of shoes that are a year old; they may even have a wrinkle or two, but they will be scrubbed to the max. Either male or female, dusty feet will be the first thing another black person will notice if you try to approach them or stand around them. If you are a male with dusty feet, you can hang it up on trying to holler at a black girl. You get no respect in the room when you have dusty feet.

YOUNG: AND HAVING FAITH N THE HOOD

This obsession with the way one looks has grown mad in the black society. Every since I was in the middle school, I've seen kids that try to be the first with the newest Jordan's, the highest rated designer brands, and the first to have what the other teens didn't have.

Popularity is not gained off of who has the highest grades, or who's the most behaved. It's not based off of who's more likely to succeed in life. It's based off of the best dressed. A male doesn't even have to be attractive; as long as he can dress and stay in the latest fashions. A female will borrow and steal just to stay current. Black society also spend thousands of dollars per year to buy fake hair to rock different hairstyles every week. Black people have become the leading consumers of fashion in the world. They thrive off of the attention. Fresh fashions will change your whole life status in the black community. To impress someone, you have to stay fresh.

Black society can buy up all the latest fashions mentioned in popular R&B and Rap music, but continue to have high dropout rates, lack of education, single parent homes, and high rates of teenage pregnancies. Maybe they are looking too good for their own good. All of this money spent on fashions, but who is investing in property, or stocks and bonds for their children's futures? Does anyone even care about that or is it better to just look and good and pretend it's all good? People will spend government checks, child support, school money, steal, and more just to stay up on the latest fashions. They don't even mind being broke just as long as they look good.

What a foolish way of thinking. It is a backwards way of thinking. If someone would give you and I five hundred dollars apiece; you would be thinking shoes and clothes, and I would be thinking investing in a product to sell that would double or triple the money I just received. Then I would reinvest again, but have a profit to spend on whatever it is that I wanted. *You would just be out of money*. Don't get me wrong, it is very important to be presentable. It brings out beauty and confidence. But, it can be abused when it becomes an obsession and too much money and thought is invested into it for no particular reason, except want and desire. This is especially for those that have a closet full of clothes that they've only worn once and had no initial intention on wearing again. When priorities aren't straight, and you aren't gaining and moving forward, who really cares how good you look? Everyone can also see that you aren't going anywhere. I'm just saying.

The Distracting Facebook Epidemic

Facebook has been a great way to reconnect with old friends from the past and keep up with everyone else. We have learned more about each others' lives. With certain people we have learned a little bit more than we should know. We share pictures and messages with people that we would never have been able to reach before. I too have been a loyal member of the facebook epidemic.

It's almost like every time you pick up your cell phone or get on your computer that you find yourself logging onto Facebook. Then you find yourself scrolling people's business for the next twenty plus minutes without even realizing or planning on it. When you're bored, you find yourself spending hours on Facebook. It has become such a distraction to nosy people and attention seekers that business doesn't get handled correctly or on time, and your kids lose the attention that they need behind it. People have their faces buried into their phones everywhere nowadays staring at their virtual world that is planted within the Facebook platform.

The attention seekers are the messy ones. The girls are the worst in my opinion. These are the ones who post the half-naked pictures just to get all of the *likes*. Their heads are so gassed up that now they think that they're really somebody special in this virtual world of theirs. They do nothing special in reality, but behind the Facebook platform they are superstars. Now that they have this status they are dedicated to posting anywhere from seven to ten posts or more a day. It's usually the ones that were unpopular, unattractive, and had the lowest self confidence and self esteem. They are easily gassed up by *likes* and *comments* on their half-naked photos. They feel that they have finally become somebody that actually no one really even knows. The guys get thirsty in their inboxes because they don't really do much but have time to fantasize over photos on Facebook. This still makes the ladies feel special like people want them. Imagine that though, what could he really want from someone who he knows nothing about?

Facebook members have destroyed their own relationships, as well as other peoples' relationships. They have been the cause of many internet and street dramas. People are so distracted by it that they actually take the content too seriously and personal. People are embarrassing themselves by displaying too much about themselves. Others are trying to portray themselves as something that they're not. Everyone doesn't use Facebook the same way though. You will know immediately who the *drama queens and kings* are, as you will see their name associated with negativity just about every time you log on.

Folks need to wake up and realize that they are displaying themselves negatively to the world. Posting your slutty business, or your alcoholism, or your every day/weekend party life, or your drug addictions is the ignorance that is the reason that the black society is laughed at and stereotyped the way that we are. I can honestly say that in the five years that I've been a member of the Facebook community I've never once posted anything negative at all. Nor have I ever posted any statuses using curse words. It's just some things you have to control. You never know who is watching you speak ignorantly and they are characterizing you as the person that you portray. You can't get mad when you are treated as you portray yourself to be. A few of our black women have disgraced themselves on Facebook. Seeing our queens being disrespectful and filthy are the reasons our men won't strengthen up. They even allow others to disrespect them. These women should definitely set better examples than they do. It's too many ignorant men out there for our women to be so ignorant. Skip the attention, set the example. And for the ones that post all of the drunken club pictures up at night and the very next morning post the *'#1 mommy'* pictures with the kids, no one respects you for that. You look and sound stupid and we all are laughing at you, but we feel sorry for the babies. Everyone notices that you leave your kids every weekend to get drunk and party. Let's start focusing on having more out life than living our lives distracted by what each other are doing on social networks. A lot of people have too much time on their hands, and while you're pretending to be all good, you're making yourself look bad while poisoning your followers with your everyday ignorance and nonsense. If you are really a good parent use the time you put into Facebook and give it to your children. They need it more than we need to see your daily foolishness.

Societies Plan For Black Youth

Whether you understand it, or whether you see it or not, young black youth have been playing right into the plan that society has set for young black people. It must make the world leaders very excited to see that after all of the work and efforts and struggles and death that our ancestors and black leaders endured to gain our freedoms; they still have managed to keep the majority of black people low class and still enslaved.

Think about who has flooded this country with drugs. Now think about who they gave the drugs too; in order to flood the black communities, and assist in destroying black people. It was the black people. Loads of government dollars funded drug dealers. The dealers created the addicts. The dealers became addicted to the money, and the addicts became addicted to the drugs. Once they'd accomplished that task, then they would put the dealer and the addict in jails and prisons for committing a crime. You can take the drugs and money from the addict, but they stay addicted. You can take the dealers freedom and money away, but they will stay addicted to the lifestyle and money. Therefore, they continue it when they get out. The saga continues as the drug life is glorified and glamorized in music and there are youth who are seeking attention for their drug addictions; while flaunting their favorite drugs to the public. This must be an exciting view to the world leaders.

In the 1960's, a program known as (SNAP) was reintroduced. This program is known to many as '*Food Stamps*.' You could qualify for this program by having a poverty level income and by removing the father from the household. This program became a huge success.

Women no longer had to work to feed their kids anymore. They didn't need to depend on a man/father to make this happen either. All they had to do was stay broke and live. The kids no longer had daddy in the house though. Although mother was broke and couldn't afford to buy her kids nice clothes, a nice house, a decent car, or provide them with continuing education she was able to feed them and had gained her independence. Now that is just great. Now forty years later, a young girl gets pregnant and runs straight to the government for assistance. They have been taught that they don't have to work and nor do they have an immediate desire too. They have been taught to find comfort at a low class/poverty level. Neither do they feel the need to have the father in their household because for the last forty plus years, that's the way the black households have been surviving. Single parent homes are constantly rising in numbers. Young black children live in hoods and ghettos with no fathers, mothers that only want to do minimal, and they are eventually raised to repeat this same cycle. This must really make the world leaders excited to see that this plan put into play by President Lyndon Johnson really worked.

Black on black crime has been high for decades as well. Black on black murders and gang activity has terrorized the black community. This sums up as prison time for the person who committed the crime and death for the victim. It is a win-win situation when you want to control the black population. Just sit back and watch them kill each other.

What's worse about this is the glorification that is regularly publicized through social media. Facebook members post alcohol pictures glamorizing alcoholism amongst our youth. They post pictures of drugs. They post reckless statuses that glorify their addictions so that the world can see it and imitate. They glamorize living a single life. They glamorize drama. Fatherless homes are glamorized. Black youth that are at poverty level incomes are posting regular pictures of '*the party life*,' depicting a society of '*drunken zombies*.' All of these things are being absorbed by those alike and the youth that just watch and listen. It's creating a chain reaction of weak-minded followers that can't wait to imitate because they think the person they see and hear is cool and what they are doing is cool. These occurrences play right into the plan that was designed for us to begin with. There are equal opportunities for us to succeed, but as long as the masses of black people fall into these unrecognized traps, we will stay trapped up in crime, poverty, and addictions. We will never come up. We will train others to do just as bad, and they will too. Only the strong person will take advantage and survive through this flood of ignorance that has actually become a lifestyle that people don't recognize as wrong simply because everyone is doing the same and thinking the same. There are really groups out here that are watching our progressions and our downfalls and they are planning against us as well. It has a lot to do with taking your money, probably more than it has to do with your downfalls. Poverty level people are known to spend money foolishly to begin with. Therefore, they are attacked the hardest. Believe it or not, low income people will spend all that they have just to look rich. Besides that, they are more prone to committing crimes. So the courts, the county, and the state wind up taking all of their money. Just look at the eye that sits inside that pyramid on your money. In order to make that money, our ways and actions have to be watched and monitored. We only make matters worse by making them rich by buying up all the latest fashions. They are regularly advertising this junk right to us. We are already broke, but we are spending the most money on the most ridiculous things they can sell to us. We have to stop allowing these people to breaks us. We are the ones making ourselves look bad by falling into every trap that they set for us. Get yourself educated about the world around you.

Distracting Us For What?

We have been distracted by so many things over the past decade. The use of technology has been a primary way to get us to not pay attention to what is happening around us. So many changes have taken place over the years that the government doesn't want everyone to zoom in on, and they are very successful at putting these distractions in place and focusing our attention on anything but the real truths.

There are a large percentage of young people that have no idea about the politics in America and the surrounding world. So many changes have happened right before our eyes that if you don't pay attention, they will affect you greatly without your knowledge. Changes to laws, healthcare, benefits, programs, leadership, and society happen all of the time. But the young society seems to be so caught up and distracted by things that take place on the internet. The largest distraction has been social networks. Besides the news media, television has also been a major distraction. There has been a creation of captivating entertainment superstars, television shows, movie channels, and music industry giants; along with a webpage and Youtube video for everyone and everything. All of these things are designed to take your mind off of the real time changes that are affecting us every day. The sad part is the information that we are missing is readily available to us more than we know. You can actually watch the House, the Congressional, and the Senate meetings live on various cable channels. You can see and hear the people that are making the decisions over your life. But not very many are tuning in. Becoming like the next trending superstar is the only thing that seems to be on the minds of the youth.

YOUNG: AND HAVING FAITH N THE HOOD

Instead of following what's going on around them, people would rather follow celebrities on Twitter. The belief that you don't need to pay attention to the politics until it directly affects you is wrong. No matter what it is, it impacts all of us directly in some kind of way. You can't forget that we all pay taxes and fund this government. We shouldn't just sit back and allow them to do whatever, and make whatever changes they want without paying attention to what it is that they are doing.

All kinds of things are put into place to distract us. You can't believe all news media. The news media is controlled by the higher powers as well. TV and internet, advertising the latest trends, the latest fashions, and video games are some of the reasons that people stay worried about standing out amongst their peers. They have no desire to know the truths around us. Without your input, without your protests, and without your votes you have no voice in the decision making. Therefore, the government is even more entitled to do as they please and shape the world into whatever it is that they want it to be. A distracted society of people can't change what they know nothing about.

Breakdown of the Illuminati

There are a lot of internet/social media junkies that holler about the illuminati. Most don't have a clue what they are even talking about. Nor do they know who the illuminati are. They listen to other people that also don't know what they're talking about and now they strongly believe the illuminati are rappers, entertainers, and movie stars. Most of them even believe the illuminati are one huge group of people. They are hyping these beliefs up and discussing them all wrong.

I want to give a basic breakdown of a few of the groups that create the illuminati because it is important, as it involves the world around us and really needs to be understood. The world around us is not a game and people make themselves look and sound stupid elaborating on things that they know nothing about. They are just hearing things from the internet and different people and spreading their own twists and opinions.

I won't elaborate on these groups in full, as the information on each group is more complex and would require a separate book. Since everyone is savvy enough, all of these groups can be searched on the internet and local libraries. I personally recommend you picking up a book if you want the most accurate information.

The star that represents the illuminati has six points. Each point represents a different group. In the middle of the star is an eye. The same eye that is spotted on the dollar bill that is inside the pyramid. The name 'illuminati' represents these groups as a whole. The term 'illuminati' comes from the term 'illuminate;' which means "to light up," or "to be able to see" in other words. These groups are the ones that are keeping an eye on us, while monitoring and controlling the world around us.

The six groups that represent the illuminati are 'The Bilderberg Group,' 'The Tri-Lateral Commission,' 'The United Nations (UN),' 'Skull N Bones,' 'The Council on Foreign Relations (CFR),' and 'The Club of Rome.' These groups have their own group of members, with some representing one or more of these groups. These are some of our world leaders who make the rules. Most of them are quiet groups with secret agendas. These groups are the ones who pick our leaders and make the changes in our world. They start and end wars. They also are associated with the big names that we are very familiar with. They meet in sometimes secret locations throughout the world, a few times out of the year, and some more than that. Other groups and rituals have been associated with the illuminati such as: 'the Freemasons' and attendees of the 'Bohemian Grove.' The attendees of the Bohemian Grove, is a group of men that have been known to worship a very large owl, sacrifice a burnt baby, and engage in homosexual activities.

These groups are real and they are active. Skull N Bones is a college group based out of Yale University. This group is said to be the molders of our future presidents including; George Bush Jr., and current Secretary of State, John Kerry. When it comes to rappers and entertainers, of course there are ties to these people. These groups own the entertainment business and the news media. They are the ones that pick what is broadcast to the public. They create the megastars. This is why it is better to read a book than to learn from the news and the internet. The books have the real information. TV and internet just distract you from wanting to seek the information from the books. As sure as we have it available on the internet and television, that content that you are absorbing is being controlled from these powers most of the time. These groups know that it is easy to get you to believe whatever it is that they want you to think if they broadcast it to the masses using entertainment news, celebrities, movies, and music. That's why we are fed continuous news coverage of terrorists and wars. They want us to believe that we really have threatening enemies. But truthfully, they are the ones that are making the enemies. They want us to listen, see, and absorb more sex, violence, and turmoil. If you stop at believing that entertainers are the illuminati, then you will look no further and blame Jay-Z and Beyonce for all of our problems and changes. All of these things make money. It makes lots of it too. When you act on what you are seeing and hearing, you are making these big named companies and governments rich off of you going to jail, becoming addicts, making babies, and whatever other reckless behaviors you adopt. Wake up people. Think about something, if you were ever beefing with somebody would you be able to negotiate with them and beef at the same time? NO. So, how is it that we can be at war with a whole country, but the leaders of those two countries are communicating and negotiating on television peacefully even while the guns and bombs are currently bursting? It seems to be something wrong with that picture right there.

Pay Attention to Politics

The world around is never going to be a play thing. The talk on the news that we hurry up and turn the channel from to our favorite distracting TV shows is not just jive talk. It also shouldn't be ignored. There is a lot that is mentioned on the news and the radio that is mumbo jumbo and doesn't apply to us, but be sure to take the time to recognize real information before tuning it out. We must pay attention to politics so that the world around us doesn't change without us knowing those changes.

I've heard too many times, "*I don't care, I don't care.*" But the second a change hits too close to home and appears on your Facebook newsfeed, everybody that '*don't care*' forms an opinion. Not only that, they have no idea what they're even talking about, nor do they realize the root of the news that they are hearing. When quiet as kept, this news has been getting discussed and broadcast for weeks, months, and years. What wound up happening is, '*I don't care*' let the trouble walk right in the house before spotting it coming up the street first. Everybody closes their ears and eyes. They switch the channel to their favorite distraction. '*I don't care*' misses out on who was elected to be our state governors, our state senators, whose running the House, whose running the Senate, and who our world leaders are. A great amount of people have no idea who our Vice President is. The only thing that interests them is the '*Illuminati;*' and they don't even know what that is.

We can't ignore who is making all the decisions for us. We are given the right to listen in, participate, and vote on proposals and laws. We can easily communicate with mayors and governors offices. These people are public figures. Their information is not secret or hidden, it is public. We are the ones that choose not to though. This makes it easier for them to have hidden agendas and secret policies. Too many people don't think they care until it walks right in the front door. It's sad because '*I don't care*' is the biggest complainer about not being able to get a job or not being able to rise from poverty level. They don't understand the judicial system. They wonder why they can't seem to come up. The reason is because you choose not to pay attention. There are programs, grants, and opportunities that would help you get ahead; that you will never know about. You don't choose to search out these types of resources. You didn't even know that you could write your mayor or your governor and make requests for new programs that you may qualify for, and for help with virtually anything that has to do with the state or county. People have literally freed loved ones from jail by calling the mayor's office when there was a flat out injustice involved. '*I don't care*' would never think to do something like that. They don't even know that that is a possibility.

You may not care about political discussions on FoxNews, or about a typhoon in China, nor do you have to care about all of it. But you should definitely look at and listen to talk of changes in healthcare, recent county and state laws, funding for schools and other important organizations, justice systems, and more. If our governor or president is in talks about important issues you should want to know about what, about when, and about why. Too much time is being spent tuning into our favorite distractions. Although these are great entertainment in our leisure time, they are only entertainment. They are not dealing with the serious facts of life. And the more you indulge in nonsense and foolishness, the more of a fool you will become to reality.

Allowing God to Guide Your Life

The best. Not one of the best. The best decision that I've ever made in my life was accepting and allowing God to guide my life. I was nineteen years old and incarcerated for a promise and a lie that I had made to God. I had known Him for many years prior to this, but I guess I didn't take Him as serious as He should be taken. I easily took Him in and took Him serious after that. At that moment when all of this occurred, He proved Himself very real to me.

Everyone has a testimony. Everyone actually has several testimonies. Some don't even know what their testimonies are. Without elaborating too much about how I was incarcerated for lying to God, I'll just briefly explain.

I was getting out of control with drinking alcohol and I caught a charge, got convicted, and got put on probation. Soon after this, I did too much drinking one night and had gotten into some more trouble. I went home and said a prayer, making an actual promise to God that if He would get me out of this problem I would never drink again. He got me out of the problem, and I lied. I started drinking again almost immediately. Two weeks later, I caught a public intoxication charge which violated my probation. I didn't come home again for six months. I was devastated. But, the sit-down allowed me to realize what it was that I did wrong. Instead of being down on myself I recognized God as a real Father and I embraced Him as such. I started studying the bible for myself. I started praying only genuine prayers. I learned about fasting. I started to feel Him working on me directly.

I must have read something in the bible about allowing God to guide your life because that is all that I wanted to do. I understood that He became the captain and I would no longer be doing anything or making any decisions on my own. As long as I believed and had faith in Him and His plan for my life I would not need to be afraid or worry about anything ever again. I understood that I was still subject to the issues and problems that people faced, but He would not let me fall or put anything on me that I couldn't bear. I understood that I belonged to Him, and His plan is now my plan also. My plans are gone because they never have been His plans. I couldn't wait to ask for this change in my life, and I did so immediately. There was nothing greater to me than to allow the Creator of life to take control of my life. And that is exactly what happened. If there was anything that I ever wanted, I made sure that I went to God for it. If He didn't provide it, I knew it wasn't meant for me. Anything that I had gained I thanked Him for it. I recognized that He wanted me to have it. Anything that has ever happened to me, whether good or bad, I embraced the experience to find the lesson and/or meaning of it. It was never hard to find either. The hardest thing that I had to decipher was after my first child had passed while I was twenty two years of age and I couldn't rest until I knew where she was. He provided my answer in a dream within about two weeks after I buried her. I think about her every day, but I no longer worry about her whereabouts.

I never worry about finding jobs, finding out, or finding myself. I have still faced many downfalls and challenges, but I have been very well taken care of. The only requirement is effective communication (prayer) and unconditional love. And I've known since I was nineteen that the love and acceptance would never be a problem. And it never once has been. The communication has fallen short at times on my part though. I've noticed some rocky roads when that has occurred. But once I pick back up on communicating it is smooth sailing. Never have I felt that He was not there through any situation, ever. Without the communication I've felt myself trying to do my own thing. Therefore, what I'm trying to do doesn't receive the blessing from God.

It is entirely up to you. It's the greatest decision that I've ever made. I feel like I have my own personal bodyguard. I have my own personal coach. I have my own personal manager. I have my own personal referee. I have my own best friend. I have my own personal Savior.

Power of Prayer

Prayer was introduced to me as a young child. Specifically, around the time I was eight years old. My father used to pray with me, mostly during his most trying times, which initially introduced me to the power of prayer.

Not only did my father introduce it to me, my paternal grandfather did as well. Seeming to be hereditarily passed down to my father, I was able to take in meaningful prayers to God that consisted of enhanced voice tones, deep concentration, biblical wordplay, and tears. Lots of tears. In fact, going to church with my grandfather and seeing him end every service with prayer, while shouting tearfully and speaking in terms that I could barely understand allowed me to further understand how powerful and meaningful prayer is. As a child, prayer never seemed to impact my life that much, so I thought. I often heard people say that they were praying for us, but I didn't care too much about that. I was taught to pray, but I only prayed to try to weasel a few gifts out of God that I was told I could get if I prayed for it. I never seemed to receive them though.

But I did learn about the significance of prayer at the right time in my life though. Becoming a nineteen year old that was already out on my own; I thank God that I was no stranger to prayer. I started to see that I was going to be putting prayer to good use sooner or later. I started to go through difficult situations that prayer was going to be the only solution for. Prayer was defined to me as sending your worries to the Most High and allowing Him to guide you through any situation that you may have. Not only that, prayer was about giving thanks, interceding into others' situations, expressing love for God, acknowledging blessings, asking for forgiveness for sins, asking for blessings, and asking for guidance and protection from the evils of the world.

I started to see prayers being answered right before my very eyes. I learned the power of God by praying. Although I have many testimonies to His power, the largest one that I share the most is just before I lost my first child to heart disease. I prayed and prayed daily that God keep her alive as she lie in the hospital on various life supports for over five months. I tried any and everything with doctors that I felt would work to strengthen her heart. Nothing worked though. She was actually gone. God was keeping her alive because I was praying that He *wouldn't* take her every day. In fact, her passing was the last thing that I could fathom. But God had already known that He was taking her long before I did. He kept her alive until I couldn't take her suffering anymore. Instead of me continuously hoping she would get better, I shifted my mind to recognizing her suffering. Others had hinted to me that I was allowing her to suffer without being blunt and risking upsetting me. I then laid my head on the window in her hospital room and I remember telling God that, *"if you want to take her, then you can take her."* In less than five hours, she was gone. I didn't blame God at all. I learned more about the power of God and the power of prayer.

I have experienced points in my life when I didn't pray, even while I knew its power. Eventually, it just led to faith shake ups, wrong turns, and mistake after mistake. Soon, I just lost track of God in my life. I've landed in pretty difficult situations as a result, because I seemed to be trying to move on my own, and I knew better than that. I've witnessed and used several types of prayer methods. I've shouted praises, silently prayed, prayed on bended knee, and even prayed while driving. None of these were any better, or any less effective than the next. Any prayer method was better than not praying at all. I believe He receives them all the same. I would just say be careful what it is that you are praying for, and have the right intentions. Don't play with God with your words. Also, don't allow just anybody to pray for you. Everyone doesn't have good intentions. But those that do have your best interest at heart, that is more prayers that are sent up for your well being. This is always beneficial for you.

Do I Really Need To Attend Church?

I can remember being raised in the church as a child and getting used to the routine about as much as I was used to the routine of attending regular school. I can recall my elders attending; and some that didn't attend. I most certainly remember my paternal grandfather praying and installing the importance of church attendance and membership. Attending church was just a routine to me though. It was a routine that I couldn't recall gaining much from as a child. I don't recall ever attending as a teenager, except a handful of times with my girlfriend's family. It wasn't until I was an adult and found a church home of my own that I'd realized how important attending church is; and the impact that it did have on me as a child.

As an adult that attended church, I didn't feel out of place. I felt as if I'd already had this understanding of God, the usual Baptist church Sunday service process, and also familiar with the literature that was being taught. It was easier to accept God into my life, and I found it easy to pray. I was raised in the Baptist church and all of my family shared the same Baptist church beliefs.

Upon regular attendance, I found myself catching the same '*Holy Ghost*,' developing the same '*church-goers glow*' on my face and having the desire to want to be more involved in whatever way that I could. I easily felt the spirit of God working on me from day to day. I felt even more blessed and open to opportunity and advancement than I had ever felt before. I felt love from the pastor and the congregation. I felt like I was getting a spiritual fulfillment.

Then somehow, being the over-thinker that I am, I started to doubt that being religious and having the viewpoints of only one person that was delivering the same message and opinions to hundreds of people at the same time was a little unusual. I also wondered how there is only one God, but there are hundreds of different churches in one city alone. I felt if there was only one God there should only be one Word. There shouldn't be all of these different viewpoints that all stem from one book. I started to look at the church as big business ushering in heaps of money from members that are paying for someone to guide their minds with their own personal views and interpretations of the bible and the ways that they felt we should be living. I looked at how they stated that we were giving the money to God. Being required to give a certain percentage of your earnings puzzled me. I understood that the pastor deserved to be paid for delivering the Word, and that the Kingdom needed to be maintained, but I witnessed large sums of money being ushered out of members to fund other projects while members were led to believe that they would not receive blessings from God if they didn't give to these project ideas. I believed that the pastor should have been straight up by teaching that we are to pay tithes and offering for the Word that we are receiving and to maintain the Kingdom. I would've respected that more. I never really noticed much community involvement by the church; unless it was to boost membership of the church or the pastor's image and reputation. Most church functions only involved that particular church and its members. The leaders of the church didn't strike me as the leaders of the community that I would have expected them to be. They led only their church and kept important, community changing information inside of the church. For these reasons, and some others, I decided to stop attending. I could do my own studying. I could say my own prayers. I could feed my own spirit. In fact, I was a leader myself and I could start my own ministry that would reach out in places where I felt the church failed at.

A problem that I faced with that decision is that that was only *'my'* decision. I may have been able to spiritually feed myself, but my family (wife and kids) couldn't. They needed that guidance and those teachings from the church in order to keep their spirits fulfilled. What I gained from my church attendance as a child empowered me later on in life, and I didn't want my children to lack that same empowerment. They would be able to later grow and make up their own minds. It was my responsibility right now though to keep my family fed, and I rediscovered why attending church was important. I realized how the attendance of all of the members empowered and fed the spirits of everyone else that attended. We feed off of each other. In fact, not everyone that attends church is weak in faith. Even the strong needs to come back and power up at times, as we all fall short at different periods in our lives. If you have the ability to interpret the Word of God on your own and remain full of the Spirit that is great, but with a great church home and great leadership it is hard to deny the positive effects that church attendance has on your life and your family's lives. God bless the church.

Doing Good Deeds; While Living All Wrong

It comes a time when God's people will experience an overwhelming feeling that comes over them that is full of love for our Father. It is a deep feeling of joy. It is an instant surge of faith. Some of us develop visions of how to keep these feelings alive by doing good deeds. I think it is safe to say that you have been '*star struck.*'

It's no surprise that when we are overjoyed by God's love and many blessings, most of us join a church and search for a way to become active. Others testify to others about how God is intervening in their lives. They share their personal blessings. Some start their own ministries through prayer groups, through music, and other various forms of ministering. But believe it or not, some people can get so caught up in ministering to other people that they forget about what is going on with them personally and actually lose sight of God in their own lives. They overlook how wrong they are living because they are caught up in helping others come closer to God.

I once had fallen victim to starting a music ministry and getting so caught up in delivering a righteous and spiritual message to my followers and listeners, that I felt I was spared being held accountable for my own wrongdoings. I felt as if the things that I was doing wrong were only observed by me and overlooked by God. I'm thinking, *"He sees and hears the messages and positivity that I am displaying and promoting to His people. Surely I can get away with this and that in exchange for my good deeds that I am doing to uplift Him."*

Sadly, I got away with a lot of the things that I wanted to keep hidden. I was able to hide in the shadows and tell myself that I wasn't being detected. The truth is, out of respect for me and my ministry, people didn't say anything about what they thought of me as a person. They did witness all that I was doing wrong and discussing it amongst each other though. It turned out that there was no need for others to say anything. Nor was it necessary for God to intervene. I was soon going to destroy myself and I was going to recognize the cause of that destruction once it happened. Living a bad lifestyle was starting to eventually show. It started to outweigh all of the good deeds that I was doing. And when it did, everyone knew. It showed all over me, and those around me started to speak on my destructive nature that I was trying to hide before.

The worse came when the ministry that I'd started and nurtured started going downhill. It went downhill about as fast as I could start losing faith in it. I noticed that the plans that I'd made for the ministry would fail one by one. My ministry was hanging on by life support. Now the good deeds that I felt I was doing for God and His people really meant nothing. It was no longer moving forward. It was active and relevant; but at a stand-still. In fact, my life had spiraled out of control gradually from the wrongdoings that I had embraced. That was all that I could focus on. I was worried more about that than worrying about what I could do right.

I later sat back and learned the meaning of the saying *"faith without works is dead."* My ministry was still alive because I hadn't killed it. But it was clear that God had stopped blessing it. It was not going to prosper anymore because my deeds didn't align with the lifestyle that I was living. I was caught up in doing what I wanted to do instead. I was doing the most. You can't expect that just because you attend church regularly on Sundays, brag about your regular attendance, and do the most wrong throughout the rest of the week that you will receive all of the glory from God for attending. You must keep in mind that God doesn't owe you any favors because of your good deeds anyway. He supplies you on a daily basis regardless of what it is that you do. And He will continue to. Good deeds should be done out of love for God and His people, and followed up by a visual that aligns with the righteousness that you intend to portray. No one is perfect but reckless behavior must not get in the way, or the good deeds you are doing will become null and void.

Observing Your Life Spiraling Out of Control

If you are used to paying attention to signs from God and you have been used to paying attention to patterns that you have experienced in your personal life, you can easily observe when your life is spiraling out of control. Often times the intelligent person will notice when something isn't right or isn't working for them and they will make the necessary changes. Thus, no longer having to deal with the same results and watching your life get back on track. But, every now and then something else sends us spiraling.

Could it be that we are relapsing back into our old ways? Are we now abusing what once started out as a simple pleasure? It could be that our life is going in a different direction now that can't involve certain things that we are used to doing. We can't indulge in the same habits forever. This is a part of growing into the new you that I like to call, 'Today's You.' Growth, maturity, responsibility, and God's plan plays important roles in these episodes that can spiral your life out of control. Without the spiral you wouldn't recognize these normal occurrences as problems, and therefore you would never grow into what you are supposed to become. True enough, you are given a free will to make whatever decisions you choose regarding your life. But isn't it great that God can intervene and send you spiraling in order to get you to pay attention to a change that is about to take place in your life. These spirals come in many different forms; but the one that pays attention will recognize them when they happen. If you choose to do anything about it is left totally up to you. Pay close attention to your ups and downs. They always tell you when you are on the right and wrong tracks. Not only that, they show you what you were doing to bring you up or what you did to bring you down. Don't think of difficult times as bad times. Think of them as learning times that you needed to get you aligned and on the right track to avoid further destruction. God is giving you chance after chance to get you to recognize and make the changes so that He can move you further.

It's also important during these times not to blame God for what's going on. Look at it as *He has His eyes and hands on you*. Not only that, He loves you enough to do that. He wants nothing but the best for you and sees more for you than you can see for yourself even at this point in your life. Think about all of the difficult situations you've faced in your life before this one. Don't you wonder how you are still here and overcame all of those obstacles? Everyone, including yourself, felt like you weren't going to make it through. But by the grace of God, you did. Always think about turning your negatives into positives. There is always good that can come out of every bad situation. In fact, you wouldn't even know a good situation if you have never experienced a bad one. Getting your life back on track is entirely up to you. You are just provided with the map of what turns are the right turns and which turns lead to dead ends. Some roads used to be smooth rides but when you lost track of the direction you were supposed to go you almost were going to miss the destination. I'm sure you understand the point that I am trying to make.

Seeking Your Purpose

There is no greater feeling than knowing and understanding what God's plan is for you while you're here. There are many people that are in their middle ages that still don't understand their purpose in life. I believe it is important to seek out your purpose and work the plan. Besides, this plan that God has for you should feel like your reason for existence; and a precious gift that can define you.

I understood one thing for sure. The only thing we take from this life when we leave is our hard work. We take no one or no thing with us. We leave many things behind except our uniqueness, our efforts, our strengths, our willpower; we take these with us. Many will have similar abilities to do similar things, but there will never be another like you. In fact, we take it with us and leave it behind as works. Like art that we've composed. Even structures that we've built.

Some haven't figured out their purpose, nor do they know how. The answer is that you have to seek it from God. You have to ask Him if He hasn't already revealed it to you. Sometimes it is right there before our very eyes. Some of us are already doing what we are put here to do; and don't know it. We are blessed with gifts. There is a reason why you know how to do certain things. This is why you are passionate about doing them also. These things aren't to be overlooked by any means. The people that have the most difficulty with finding their purpose should be the ones who've noticed that they have multiple gifts. Seeking your purpose by communicating it with God will help you sort out what you should really be doing. The people who feel they aren't supposed to be working a 9-5 job all of their life probably isn't supposed to be. Ask God about the feelings that you are having; and why. Some have jobs that they have turned into careers. They are a blessing to that company. They possess the gifts that that company needs. This may be their purpose. This is why God sent them to that company in the first place. No matter what kind of job or work that it is somebody has to do it. If the product, or company, exists in this world it has to be run and maintained by somebody. There is somebody for everything that we have going on, and that just may be you. God's purpose for you may be for you to be right where you are.

Purpose isn't to be confused with dreams. And neither is it to be confused with chasing dreams. The average person doesn't have just one purpose either. At different ages and stages, God gets you ready for new things. You may not even know it at the time, but you could have been fulfilling God's purposes unknowingly. The people you help and the places you've been are a part of the plan. The things you've done have benefitted somebody somewhere. Whether good or bad, somebody has learned something. God works in mysterious ways; and He guides us where He needs us to be whether we know it or not. Dreams are more of a personal mission that you want to receive a blessing from God for. They are usually self-satisfying; but they can very well be a part of God's plan; especially when the dream involves impacting the lives of others.

Sitting around and waiting, with no communication, will just have you confused on what you are doing, or what you are supposed to be doing. God will use you wherever it is that He needs you. When you believe in God, He is already using you to carry out His plans. It is up to you to want to know how you are being a blessing to someone. We have all fulfilled many purposes that God has given us. We are right in the middle of another one. To have no purpose leaves a person no reason to be in attendance on this earth. You have nothing but your efforts and your works. Anything else is not really yours to be so proud of. You are judged by your works that you put in when you are fulfilling your purpose.

What Is Sin?

As stated before I am not a biblical scholar. I don't have all of the answers. I just logically take what I've learned throughout life and I try to help others understand and develop their own understanding of circumstances and situations that come up in life. I find myself ministering to clueless people, simple-minded people, curious people, and even difficult people. Ultimately, everyone just wants to know and try to understand life better.

So I was asked, "What is sin?" I simply explained sin as being something that you are doing that is not pleasing to God. I defined it as doing, saying, or being something or someone that YOU know in your heart is not right, whether it pertains to you or for mankind in general. Everyone was given the image and likeness of God. This is why we tend to acknowledge similar rights and wrongs. Also, depending on where you are originated from, certain things were taught to be right and other things were taught to be wrong that doesn't align with what others' in different nations consider to be right and wrong. I believe God shapes His plan for you by what you were created to understand and know. He placed you where you are from to create who you are to become. Thinking certain ways outside of what you know is right can be a sin as well. Especially since it can cause you to carry out sinful deeds. With that being said, I don't believe that sin is the same for any two people. Meaning, what's a sin to you is not a sin to me unless we both have the same right and wrong beliefs on the particular action. It's based on what you know and don't know; what you understand and don't understand as being right or wrong. If you don't understand something as being wrong, how can it be a sin to you? It is similar to children not having a sinful nature until they are able to know and feel the difference between their right and wrong actions. Therefore, they aren't condemned for what we as adults look at them and see that they're doing wrong. There was no way they would feel the right from the wrong understanding of their actions. When they do learn the right and wrong, they know when they are doing wrong and they may still do it anyway, but they feel bad about it. It doesn't matter what their age is. Once they learn the difference it makes them feel some type of way. Also, once the parents know that they know the difference it is easier to punish them for the wrongdoing. Sin is about doing, saying, or thinking what YOU know is wrong in the eyes of God because YOU know better. You may just be trying to get away with something that YOU want to do.

I believe that this is why God is forgiving of sin and no sin is greater than the next. Most of us in this country feel that it is wrong and the ultimate sin 'to kill.' But have you ever thought about the background of some killers? Did you ever think that some don't feel or wasn't raised to think that killing is wrong? Now, it may be displeasing to God, and He may have to take steps to get this 'killer' to understand that he is doing wrong. These steps are common, and include: getting shot, losing family to gun violence, imprisonment, etc. But when He does get this person to realize, is God wrong for forgiving and helping to redeem this person? I don't think so. Controversially, people feel that smoking marijuana is a sin. I personally don't believe so. I feel like the abuse of it is. In other countries, laws are different from the laws in the United States. Lots of people believe that breaking the U.S. laws is sinful. But the same law is legal in other countries. They do this 'sinful' act all day every day. So, if you feel that smoking marijuana is a sin to God, then for whatever reason you relocate to Amsterdam (where it is legal to smoke marijuana), is everyone around you sinning?

What works for the next person may not work for you. You will always see people getting away with something all of the time that you never seem to get away with. They may not understand this as wrong, or they may not have been shown that it is wrong yet? Either you, someone else, or life will let them know if what they are doing is wrong or sinful. It's up to them to take it in as such. Ultimately, it's up to each individual as to what is sin in their life. Everyone is different and God deals accordingly. So no one is allowed to judge the sin of another person. Nor can you condemn that person or those people. You have to worry only about your own sin.

JAMES 4:17—Therefore, to him who knows to do good and does not do it, to him it is sin.

The Good and the Bad

If you've ever noticed, there is a good and a bad to virtually everything. In order to get to know the good of something you have to understand how it could go bad also. In order to know what is bad you must have first known or been told about the good. Sometimes you wind up having to take the good with the bad.

People are the main subjects when distinguishing good and bad. You wouldn't know what a bad person does to make them bad if you didn't first know what good people do. Have you ever thought that what you consider to be a 'bad person' may not be what every 'bad person' sees as making them bad? They may not even consider themselves a 'bad person' because they have seen worse than them. That's who they may consider a 'bad person.' A 'bad person' to you will also know and point out things about you that don't make you a 'good person.' When you hear their points and you believe that you are a 'good person,' does that make you feel like you are a 'bad person' now? In the movie 'Scarface;' Tony made a statement saying, "You need bad guys like me, so that you can have somebody to point your fingers at." Is that what the 'good' and the 'bad' do? Do they point fingers at each other? Who tells who whether the other is good or bad? Or is it self-proclaimed? Maybe it's just based on the weight of the good or bad deeds one commits. But, the 'bad' looks down on the deeds of the 'good.' The 'good' points fingers at the deeds of the 'bad.' Not only that, the 'good' will also sometime do bad deeds and find themselves in the company of the 'bad.' The 'bad' will sometime do good deeds and find themselves in the company of the 'good.' Will the roles switch now? Is that even possible?

It seems that 'good' and 'bad' people shouldn't be labeled as such in the first place. Both have the ability to change into the other. I believe everyone has a mixture of both in them. I also believe that there are people who do mostly wicked things and do very little good. The wicked deeds that override the amount of good deeds, makes that person 'bad' in the eyes of others. But that person may not be able to fully comprehend why everybody feels that what they are doing is bad. They are just doing what they know. Pointing fingers at them only gives them recognition and the so-called 'good people' an example to teach other 'good people' what not to do. But who is really penetrating the out-casted, 'bad person's' mind into believing that they are doing something bad? Have the 'good people' explained to them the opposite of their bad deeds, which would make them better or 'good?' Or are they simply just pointing fingers, punishing them, and using them as statistics and lessons for other 'good people?' A drug dealer is considered a 'bad person' in society. They are strictly punished when they are caught; it doesn't matter who they are. But, there are drug dealers that do nothing but deal the poison, shoot people, collect and spend dirty money, don't take care of anybody but themselves, and prey on the weak. Then, there are drug dealers who also deal the poison, take care of their families, they don't kill, they share the wealth, help others every day, and do positive things in the community. It's obvious that one does more good than the other and the good outweighs the bad; but is this 'bad person' a 'good person' though? If you do deeds that label you 'bad' in society you tend to feel like the 'bad guy.' Even if you switch and start doing good you still feel and are treated like the 'bad guy.' The 'good person' that does bad deeds finds a way to feel like the 'good guy,' but once they are labeled 'bad;' that usually sticks. It doesn't matter what they self-proclaim. You can do all the good in the world but your bad will always seem to stand out more. It shows how much this world is focused on negativity instead of positivity. The 'good people' do bad deeds all the time, but they remain 'good people' until they are caught and publically exposed for the bad that they've done. Now they are 'bad.' All of your good achievements and accomplishments won't mean anything once you are caught up being what everyone labels as 'bad.'

Paying for Sin

Sin is saying, doing, and thinking things that are displeasing in the eyes of God. We acknowledge our sin, ask for repentance from God, and are supposed to turn away from such things that have caused us to sin. There is also a price to pay for sin, especially when we can't seem to stop such behavior. These payments can either be because we just intentionally won't stop or we don't understand that what we are doing is sinful and God needed to intervene to get us to realize.

People pay for sin in many ways. They even pay in ways that they least expected. Truth is, we want to hope that we are under the radar. Maybe we've gotten away with something so much that it doesn't seem likely that we will be punished. But it always tends to catch up to us. Most things that we are doing wrong, we know and understand what we are doing. Nobody really cares about the consequences while they are doing whatever it is that they're doing, especially when the consequences aren't obvious.

God has His way of getting to us though. Just when you think you are experiencing a good run you could really be suffering the consequences all along. For example, abuse of drugs and alcohol may not have gotten you into trouble with the law, but it could already be having an unseen, long term effect on your body that hasn't been revealed yet. Whatever it takes to get you to understand and repent. God will allow things to happen in our lives such as imprisonment, that will really sit you down and give you time to think and sort. Parents pay for their wrongdoings that they've done to their children, or their own parents, through their very own children. They grow older and show the same characteristics most times. So you must be careful what you do as a child and as a parent, because it comes back to you in some kind of way through your own offspring.

Intelligent people also know that it is not necessary to seek revenge on people who've mistreated them or done them wrong. A person that wishes misfortune on you will wind up allowing you to have to see their own misfortunes happen at some time and there will be nothing that they can do about it. This is why you don't fight ignorance with ignorance, and you sit back and let God take care of it. When you seek revenge you set yourself up for a payment for sin also.

Is There Really A Hell?

I have debated this subject numerous times and people have continued to question is there really a place that God sends the 'bad people' of the earth where they will burn in fire indefinitely? Is there a little devil character that's standing there with a pitchfork and welcoming the 'bad people' in to watch them suffer? I am not a biblical scholar or historian, but I do have knowledge of the bible and have studied it many times. I have learned that the bible is full of parables and metaphors.

I can't help but notice that the first sentence in the bible is "*In the beginning, God created the Heaven and the Earth.*" Where does it say that He created Hell? Surely He wouldn't allow Satan, who was said to be an angel that was removed from Heaven, to create such a place for us. Neither do I believe that the God that we have known to be a loving, gracious God would be that cruel as to create us and then let us burn in fire. It's bad enough that we have to suffer here on Earth in numerous ways whether you are 'good' or 'bad.' The fact is we weren't created to be perfect anyway. Therefore, we are born into sin. Even people that seek salvation are still sinners. It would be a shame to think that you couldn't do anything right in the eyes of God and then you would put yourself at risk of going to a place that is specifically for 'bad people,' or 'unsaved people,' on a daily basis. Why would anyone feel like they are going to Heaven then?

On Earth we suffer from and die from millions of different types of diseases and cancers. We lose people to deaths. Some people lose limbs and other body parts. We can lose our own lives in an instant to robbers, murderers, and even at our own hands. We are not safe here. We face problems all of the time that cause us to lose important valuables and people. We have hungry, homeless, and lost people. There are underdeveloped nations and dictators that control lives.

YOUNG: AND HAVING FAITH N THE HOOD

There are people that haven't even had a chance to live that are being judged, convicted, and sentenced to decades in prisons. There are sick children. There are broken families. There are constant struggles. This is what sounds like Hell to me.

I believe Hell is something that you go through while living your life. I strongly don't believe that Hell is a place. It can be based on your lifestyle or what type of conditions and surroundings you were born into. People are able to overcome and climb out of Hell. Doing things that are unpleasing to God creates a Hell for you, which is why you should stay encouraged and doing the right things that are pleasing to God. God has been known to be a jealous God that I doubt would want to cast you away to a Satan. We were all created in His image and likeness. Not even you would be so cruel to do such a thing to your own children.

When your kids are disobedient you punish them in a way that will get them to recognize their mistakes. Most likely they will get the point, they ask for forgiveness (apologize), no love was lost, and life goes on happily with a lesson learned by the child and a parent that sees more of what their child is capable of and/or learning. Never do you think as a parent that you are going to destroy your child or cast them away. You never think to kill them. You never stop loving them. So why would God do the same to you? As I say, we were created in the image and likeness of our Father. Your children were created the same. Why would you think that you love harder, or better than God loves His children? We have reason to be obedient here on Earth because we 'catch hell' for our disobedience. But it is not logical thinking to think that we go to a place and burn eternally in fire. I would probably re-read and re-interpret the scriptures in the bible that speak about Hell, and try to apply them to life here on Earth. Heaven is said to be perfect and free from all of the sins, plagues, deaths, and evils. But we definitely are experiencing all of these things right now. And just when you think it has been as bad as it can get, it can definitely get worse.

Finding Your Way Back to God

One of the most difficult times that you can face in life is after the time that you've lost track of God. I mean the time when you are no longer living your life according to His plan. This is the time when you find yourself guiding your own self through life. These are the times when you've stopped praying and your faith has started slipping away. When you get to the edge of the cliff, you start trying to find your way back to God because falling off is the next step but it is not an option.

Believers are not abnormal. Nor is it nothing new to lose sight of God at times. Although it feels as though we have lost no love for God and we acknowledge His many blessings and His existence and never doubted His love, we can still lose the direction that He is guiding our life in. The main reason for this is that the way we thought things would go may not have happened for us in the way or the timeframe that we've expected. We previously thought that we had it all figured out; may have stopped seeking God's guidance, and wound up trying to make moves without Him. Over time the mission plans worsened as we are witnessing failure after failure and can't understand why or how.

It is important to know that whatever it is that you are pressed to do with your life is a gift from God. He has the plan and the direction for you to carry out the mission. It is left up to you how you interpret and follow the directions. It can either work for you; or you can fail the mission. It's entirely up to you. God communicates with us in so many recognizable ways even when you are falling short. It is also up to you to communicate back. This is why prayer should never cease. When God has provided all of the resources at any time, you know that you are in good standings with Him and His plan. It is recognizable and you accept and give thanks. When you know what you need, and it is not being provided, you may have fallen short somewhere and need to get back in touch with God. Usually, it is something that we are doing that is unacceptable to continue God's plan and it has put a halt on our forward movement. Sometimes it is something that is about to come that may hold us back for a second. This isn't able to be seen but you will thank Him once it is revealed.

The faster we make preparations to find our way back to God, the faster we can ask for forgiveness and hopefully move forward with His plan. A lot of plans have been passed up by God because of the recipient not willing to accept that they are not in control. They refuse to be or behave as God needs them to be and behave. God's plans don't allow you to be how YOU want to be or live how YOU want to live. Once you find yourself doing those things you can hang it up for further blessings on your mission. Remember, your mission accomplishments are smaller than a mustard seed to God. They are huge and seem impossible to you though. If He gave it to you from the start, believe He meant for you to accomplish it. If it fails, it was entirely your fault. The more you hold out and try to do things on your own, without the blessings of God, watch how everything life has to put in your way gets in the way. The task becomes nearly impossible to accomplish. Your mind and time is now taken to what you need to do about everything else. Do what you can to keep your dreams alive. It is up to you if you get it or miss it.

The Value of Today's Black Man

I don't really see much difference in the young black males of today than what was evident before. What has lowered the value of today's black man the most is that they have lowered the value of today's black women. If I was to base it on the last few decades, I would be able to easily see that that was on its way to happening anyway. Black males today are an endangered species that has so much work to do to survive.

First off, it seems every young black male wants to be hard; or tough. Even the softies want to show that they have some thug in them as well. Since everybody is tough, everybody has guns. Now that they have guns, they kill each other. Black on black deaths by guns are killing young black males so much that it is embarrassing and crazy. If every black male that thought about killing another black male actually did commit the act, there wouldn't be any black males left on this earth. They can't find a way to fit into society if they don't play the hard role.

We stay losing black men to the prison system, as expected. We can't seem to figure out from the other millions of victims that the drug game is a real trap. Who do you really know that has survived the drug game without dying or going to prison behind it? Black males still have to get their heads around that type of hustle and easy money. Black society still accepts the 'dopeboy' though. It's still glamorized and women still jock the 'dopemen.' Drugs have been the largest downfall of the black male for decades. This applies whether they are the seller or the user. The new, young adults fall right into the same trap. In one night you can find them under the influence of alcohol, mollies, weed, cigarettes, cocaine, and all sorts of various drugs. The black male may always be a victim of this lifestyle.

YOUNG: AND HAVING FAITH N THE HOOD

Great numbers are still walking out of the lives of their children. They aren't screening the women that they are knocking up either. They are drinking and drugging, and seducing them in one night. They are having unprotected sexual affairs with them and not taking responsibility for the babies that result from this. They are leaving these women and the kids while repeating the process over and over.

The only time that you hear about the black male going to college is when they are plotting to gain from a school check. Black males still don't want to be educated. They would rather sell drugs. They don't seek long term employment. They just would rather cop drugs. The lack of drive to further their self is unbelievable. They love to *not know* how to do important things that life is really about. *"I don't know how to work no computers." "I ain't never had a job." "I don't know how to do it."* They think it's cool when they say that. What's even crazier is the hardest ones don't even know how to read. I'm very serious. There are grown, functioning men that don't even know how to read better than a fourth grader. They can sell drugs, count money, shoot guns, make babies, buy cars, and buy clothes but they can't even read. How can these types of men help us raise intelligent children? They hate on each other all day long. They hate on intelligent black males just because they don't have that level of intelligence. The intelligent black male is considered to be 'soft;' or 'bitch made.' They aren't 'real.' It should be that not being intellectual should be considered 'soft' and 'unreal.' But ignorance has existed for centuries and I won't be the one to act like it hasn't.

Black males wanting to be the biggest drug dealer, the biggest playa, and the biggest gangsta has been destroying us and our women/queens for the longest and it needs to stop. This is not the freedoms our ancestors and black leaders fought for. They definitely weren't fighting for a nation of illiterate, outlaw gangstas. Our women have given up on us for many reasons. Some have even decided to join the ignorance. If we want to lose these she-males, and regain our 'queens;' then we most certainly can by becoming better and striving for more. The 'gangsta' life is dying off and we are dying off with it. But we should try to save the youth under us before we lose ourselves. They are the ones that are watching what we are doing. They are the ones that are perfecting ways to become even dumber. I can't stand it when I see the actions and behaviors of some of our youth. I definitely can't stand to hear the nonsense they speak about. It makes me sick how much ignorance is absorbed and mistaken for being 'real' or 'real talk.'

The Value of Today's Black Woman

I'd always thought that one day in my life as a young black male that I'd have an old-fashioned relationship that consisted of maybe three to four children, a great job, a beautiful home, nice cars, and a loving wife that was submissive, mostly a home body, raised children with excellence, helped financially, and would love her family that she'd helped to create. That was merely a dream. And in today's society that will prove to be one of the hardest lifestyles to own since even the value of today's black woman has went on a decline.

The days are gone where black women wanted to be 'queens.' They don't even want a happy family anymore. And if they do, they take all the wrong steps and paths to ensure that happiness. They seem to live their lives as and call one another 'bitches' while struggling to prove their independence in single parent homes. A high rate of them still will go to college and get degrees, but they destroy their images and lives by chasing street dudes and having multiple children before they are fully ready. They allow these guys to suck the lives out of them. Then they become damaged and scorned. A man means nothing to them anymore and they can't wait to prove it by treating every man after him like animals. They fail to realize that the only reason they've been treated this way is because of the *type* of men that they've allowed into their lives.

Today's black woman tends to adore the single life. But what they are experiencing really isn't that single of a life. It usually consists of month after month affairs and encounters; sleeping with several men at the same time and using them for sex and money. The huge, trending topic amongst our black women today is experimenting with homosexuality. All of this occurs in the presence of the children. This glamorized lifestyle has spilled out into the public eye and now very few women attract healthy relationships and traditional families. The kids remain the victims of broken homes that no one is even attempting to build on or rebuild. It seems that women have completely done away with true love and being the rock of the family. Black men have been known to screw up a household, but he used to have a 'black queen' that would lift his spirits, show him genuine love that he couldn't resist, comfort him, care for him, and make him better while he learns the true value of the family that he has. Now the woman's attention shifts faster than the minute hand on a clock. Instead of focusing on home, our black women have become more focused on drugs, alcohol, and doing way too much partying. When women have the same value as the men it is going to result in dangerous futures for the black family. Now the women take pride in being more like and thinking like men. They want to be the fathers and the mothers. They are attracted to females physically and sexually. They speak like men. They think like men.

Although this does not apply to all women, the generation of 80's and 90's babies have changed the game over the last twenty years. The new generation will be doomed when they are raised by women with these similar qualities and values. These women don't recognize their own self worth and they have brought their value down to an all time low. You can't tell them that though, because their hair is done, their curves are right, their fashions are tight, and their game is tighter. But when you do get the chance to know them they all sound misguided, ashamed, and lost. And they very much are. They are struggling from the decisions that they've made in the past and the consequences that have followed. So they hide the pain by drinking and smoking in excess. They stop caring about themselves. They barely want to take care of their children. They dog out men and blame men. They teach other women to be the same way. I hope and pray that our 'queens' come back. I pray that these evil spirits would vanish. Men will never become better if our women become weaker.

Becoming the Man/Woman That You Desire To Be

If you are anything like me you've known since a young age what type of life you desired to live and what type of man/woman that you desired to be. You were just waiting on the right time and the right person to bring out that person so that you can not only impress them, but impress yourself as well. Becoming that person was just as much of a dream as it was to be whatever it was that you wanted to be professionally.

Over the years of adulthood I've dealt with several lasting relationships and still found myself not fulfilling that dream. Either I thought that they weren't worthy enough to receive that person, or I just simply wasn't on the right track to portray that person. Eventually, I stopped having the desire to be that person. After being cheated on, lied to, misled, and hurt over and over again I felt like no one was worthy enough to see that person that I could be. The outcome was that throughout any of the encounters that I've had, I remained cold-hearted. I also grew colder and colder to all personalities. This was even if someone gave me the desire back to bring that person out. I still never chased the feeling again. I felt in the back of my mind that they would only hurt me later and make me regret putting forth any effort. And believe it or not, they usually did.
It wasn't until later that I'd realized that I wasn't getting any younger. I had to be the person that I desired to be whether the relationships were good or bad. Maybe, by me staying the same person that I've always been, this has been the reason that I kept attracting the same encounters. Maybe no one would be what I needed them to be for me without me being who I needed to be for me first. Maybe they were waiting on me to be the person that I claimed to be.

Where would I start though? I would start with ridding myself of all of the bad habits that this 'new person' could not portray. I would start with thinking of how 'this person' is supposed to think. I want to change my appearance and dress how 'this person' is supposed to dress. I want to talk how 'this person' is supposed to talk. These things will all lead to me doing what 'this person' is supposed to do. I want to walk how 'this person' is supposed to walk. I want to act how 'this person' is supposed to act. I want to feel how 'this person' is supposed to feel. After all of this, the actions that I expect to naturally fall into place will. The company that I keep will change. The people that I attract will change My needs and wants will change. My God will bless me differently and provide for me accordingly People will recognize me differently. I will look different. I will feel changed. I will be the person that I have always desired to be, and I will be proud to be that person.

I will have a new journey with God. My past will no longer repeat itself. My children will not easily become victims of my old ways and actions. I will be renewed and ready to proceed with my new life. No one would have to bring it out of me. So that would mean that new people would only know what they see currently that is standing in their presence. I can choose if I want to explain my past so that they could visualize the old me, or let it sleep in the past. This is because they will never know or imagine it if I don't tell it. I will have finally freed myself from the bondage that has held me captive for many years. Why not do it this way? I was the one that bought that life on me, so of course I should be the one to change it. Help me Lord.

What Is the Problem in Today's Relationships?

A man meets a woman. They talk. They fall in love. They spend all of their time together. They make plans to marry. They get married. They have children. They live happily ever after, with excellent children and beautiful grandchildren. They die together. All of that sounds good. But it is no longer a reality in today's society. A relationship lasts about sixty seconds. If there is any form of effective communication it may last an hour. What is the problem with today's relationships?

First off, we have grown madly attracted and lustful to the outside appearance of each other. The fashions have upgraded and become more enticing over the years. Women have clothing that reveals more curves and other features far more revealing than they ever have before. Men have style and personality that attracts the women. At first sight of each other there tends to be a sexual desire, as the world has grown more and more accustom to the era of *sexy*. With sex as the initial focus, on both ends most times, once that satisfaction has been fulfilled right away, there's a very slim chance of getting to know anything else. Once the intimacy is shared before even getting to know a person, who'd want to advance further? Everyone knows that you learn more and more about a person if you wait to share the intimacy. Because most people want the intimacy so bad that they will take the time to get to know you, therefore, they allow themselves to create a deeper intimate feeling once it does happen.

Males and females have been damaged over and over by hopping from person to person; being used for sex and later dumped, taken for money, played by players, used by users, abused, and so on. Most have started to indulge in the wild and free, single life. They aren't really single though. They still hop from person to person, further damaging their trust in the opposite sex, and they continue to sleep around with anybody they choose to. They call it single because they don't have to answer to anyone or be pressured by commitment. It's really stupid because babies and diseases come out of these reckless encounters. Now you have men and women that have different looking kids by multiple people that they don't even know, or even want to know.

Drugs, alcohol, and partying all of the time, also social networking have peoples' attention spans at an all time low. People are so high, drunk, and promiscuous that they will never be able to focus on one person. Their minds are cloudy. Their inboxes are buzzing. All of their options are wide open. You only have one mistake to make in a relationship with them before they move on to the next one whispering in their ears. No one wants to communicate with each other to make it work. It's easier to just move on because that's ultimately what they had in their mind that they would do in the beginning anyway. Too many encounters keeps someone interested, and with their own agenda, making them feel like they are making a mistake by being in a committed relationship with whoever it may be. It's always someone else on their minds while they are lying next to you like '*it's all good.*' They say that they love you, but they will leave you for the smallest disagreement. There doesn't have to be any discussion. *And they won't return*. They will be on to the next, possibly the same night.

Options are wide open and the old traditional relationships are fading away. No one feels like they need the other anymore. People are content with their independence. They are not experiencing the discipline and true love that a solid relationship can bring. Too many would rather tear apart and struggle just to be free than to build. On the flip side of that, there are way too many illegitimate kids, too many broken homes, too many strugglers pretending to be doing just fine, too much destroying of good relationships, too many snakes, too many diseases being passed around, destroyed trust in relationships and in people, too much loneliness, too much lust that is mistaken for love, too many lies, too many that come and go, and there is not enough real happiness.

Loving the Black Man

Before getting off into this subject, I must exclude the playas, the pimps, the womanizers, and the gangsta's from this topic. These are the ones that don't want to be loved. They only love and take care of themselves. Also, I will exclude all of the wanna-be's of these same types. I am only speaking about true, loving black men.

Loving the black man really doesn't take much. Black men are already taken once he finds a woman that wants to love him. The world today is filled with liars, deceivers, cheaters, and games that are even played by women so it is a great reward to find someone to love and that wants to love you back. Black men love a submissive woman that will listen to him and carry out his wishes. As this power over his queen keeps him wanting to do more and come up with more to satisfy her and him and keep their relationship anew and prospering. This is not to be confused with control, but even the submissive woman will find out that her man is making her life more satisfying and interesting. The more she is able to carry out, the better he can understand what it is that she is skilled at and what it is that she likes.

The obvious still remain the same. The way to his heart is the ability to cook a good meal, keep the place clean, satisfy intimately, and show your love for him. These tend to be natural qualities that a woman possesses, but now more than ever, it is not hard to get jammed up with a woman that is not consistent on keeping a clean house. You can definitely find many that can't shake their seasonings correctly in the kitchen. And showing love has a lot to do with understanding and learning the needs of your man. He may be a used to a certain way that requires you to make changes against what you normally do. Paying attention to him more than being distracted by friends,

72

family, and the internet keeps your focus together. If he happens to know how to cook, and you don't, don't be afraid to learn from him. This way you know what it is that he likes to eat, and how. Explain to him if you weren't taught well as a child how to cook, clean, or be considerate of individuals other than yourself. This helps him know how to guide you and keeps you from becoming frustrated with him.

A lying woman is a disastrous person to try and love the black man. This is not the way to love. Being deceitful and sneaky is a no-no. Honesty is the key to keeping the black man focused on you and only you. Black men have a known tendency to go astray when they find out that they have a dishonest woman that they can't trust. It creates the worst feeling when dealing with someone so beautiful and soft and sweet; but will lie to your face with no regard for your well being. A dishonest woman will spin a man's life and mind somewhere it has no business being. She will make him think in all of the wrong ways. This will send a relationship spiraling out of control. Stay away from dishonesty from the beginning. Stay away from cheating. This is the obvious though, and it doesn't need any elaboration. These two are not real love at all.

The black man needs support for his goals and his missions. He doesn't always want a 'yes' woman. He needs someone who can openly communicate and tell him when he is wrong, and when he may be getting on or is off of the right track. Loving the black man involves knowing how to appeal to his children, considering that they aren't shared mutually. If they are, he wants his woman to raise them right, give them the necessary attention, and be an outstanding role model and example of a top notch woman to his girls and his boys. She won't let outsiders get in the way of anything. She will have the majority of the characteristics that he has always desired to have in his woman. The black man isn't hard to love. As long as he can see that he makes you happy and that you are satisfied with him, he will continue to do what he does for you over and over again. His happiness comes from making his woman happy. He loves to do the things that make his woman love him.

Loving the Black Woman

The world is full of male and female playas and it seems that many of us aren't looking for love, but truthfully, we all want to be loved. The black woman is a natural born queen that with the right love and guidance she can be very solid, submissive, and trustworthy.

The first thing that we have to do is stop destroying the black woman from the inside. There has been too much history of lying, cheating, misleading, and using them for everything that they have that it has torn them and turned them cold. Loving a black woman is going to have to start with us understanding what black women have been dealing with from men for years and completely change that.

This means that we need to be truthful to her all of the time. Don't make things to hide. Let her truly see you as an honest man whose words are always meaningful. She will respect everything you say and feel just off of that alone. Go into the relationship with your heart set on her being your only partner. Never cheat on her. Never even let your mind drift into thinking that there is somebody better for you. If you have to be distracted by other women or you haven't filled your sexual escapades, don't try to love this woman. Wait until you've matured and are ready to commit to *one*. Don't mislead her into thinking that you want to be with her and only her when you know you are a playa. When you have a real woman around you, the wrong thing to do is to play with her heart. Men who do that add to the damage that women have now. They make it hard for good women to trust men. Don't use them for what they have. I've seen this too many times; men getting in good with women just to use them for shelter, their car, and their money. Low life men that further add to the problem of why our black women are scorned.

YOUNG: AND HAVING FAITH N THE HOOD

Love the black woman with all of your heart and she will return the love three times as much. You have to realize that a man that possesses the qualities of honesty, faithfulness, independence, strength, and willpower may be the type of man that she has never encountered in her life. Once you put that kind of magic on her, you will see the type of woman that will put her life in your hands. She will stop at nothing to please you. This is how you take a woman with a rough past, a hard rock, and turn her into a gem. They are too used to lies. They are too used to being used for sex. They are too used to giving their hearts and getting them broken. We are losing our queens every day to immature, doggish men that could care less because they will have another victim tomorrow. If you can see how deep she stares at you when you tell her how much you want to be with her, know that those same eyes have looked at someone else who've told her those similar words with a lying tongue and devilish intentions. If you have ever had the chance to wipe away her tears, wipe away the chance for anyone else to ever make her cry again. She wants to know that you respect her and care about her feelings. She wants to know that you will love her children. She wants you to protect her. She wants you to trust and believe in her. Loving the black woman isn't complicated at all. As long as you don't give her a reason to distrust you, you will receive her heart. Those that play games make the relationship that much more complicated. And even still, she stands by your side. But never take her kindness for a weakness. Just know that she wants to give you the benefit of the doubt. Loving the black woman involves heavy communication. She loves to listen, and she loves to be heard. She loves to plan with her man. She loves to be seen with her man. Ultimately, she doesn't want anyone else except her man. Try to never take loving a black woman lightly. If all men take these things into consideration and apply it to just one lucky lady, the lifestyles and statuses of some of the cold-hearted women will change. They will go back to being our 'queens' instead of feeling like the black man is so far gone that they will not ever learn how to love them right. If the black man would quit lusting and wanting every woman that he sees as attractive, he may learn how to appreciate our beautiful, black women. He may learn how to love her right.

Loving the Black Child

As we know, kids love us just because of who we are. It doesn't take much to gain the love of a child. They are the reasons and the ways that a lot of us have learned to love in the first place. They are our first true love and the first true best friend that we have ever had. They are the love and the best friend that would never leave us; for any reason. But we have to make sure that the black child is loved correctly.

Let's just say that we already know that naturally we are going to provide clothing, shelter, and food for the child as our first sign of love for our child. We are going to make sure that they get to school and that they have the tangible items that they need. But loving the child mentally and emotionally is often overlooked and they cause a child to be raised wild. See, you can have the best dressed, well fed, best house-having child in the school or family, but what is that when they are not even trained on the basics like: how to clean themselves properly, dress themselves, tie their shoes, or speak with manners. There are children who have reached the second and third grades that haven't even learned these basics.

When you are stuck on doing everything for your child, and not allowing them to learn to do basic things on their own, that is not the way to love your child right. You are crippling them. Children are raised day to day, year to year to be able-bodied adults. They are not raised to be kids. If you continue to hinder their growth by making up excuses as to why they aren't ready to do certain things for themselves you will find yourself with some teens and adults that are way too dependent. If you see all of the other kids their age doing certain things for themselves you can best believe yours should be ready too, unless there is some type of physical or mental disability.

YOUNG: AND HAVING FAITH N THE HOOD

The problem is there are lazy parents who don't have the patience to allow their child time to learn important basics. If you want to teach your six year-old how to brush their teeth, don't wait until one hour before the school bus comes to teach them. Teach them when there is plenty of time for you to train and for them to learn. He/she has plenty of energy all day. Channel it away from all of the playing. The child needs to be taught early in life about strangers, and right and left, and emergency calls, and parent's phone numbers, and many more things that they are very capable of learning.

Loving the black child involves keeping them involved with both parents. Unless one leaves, and it is out of your control, the child needs to know why and how they think, act, and feel the ways and things that they do from both sides. The best children come from two parents that are actively involved. These are the happy children. They are the smart ones. They are the ones that have the highest chance of becoming exceptional adults. Not only that, it needs to be two parents that have the child's best interest in mind always. Not the back and forth, fighting and bickering, and can't get along parents. This is not loving the child right.

Loving the black child involves keeping a clean and safe environment for them as well. The kind where the house stays clean, the atmosphere is friendly, love is always in the air, it is drug and alcohol free, there is room to play, there is room to grow, and lessons and basics are taught and learned. Every child deserves this type of loving environment to grow healthily in. When a parent, or parents, keep drug addicts, alcohol, and dealers around who start and talk about drama all day, curse uncontrollably in front of the kids, have a negative influence, and let kids just run wild, this is not the way to love a child right.

The kids are forced into this environment because they are the helpless ones. They grow up doing and thinking all of the wrong things because of this. They act like fools in school because of this. It's the parent's fault when this happens though. If you can say that you have a 'bad child' you need to know initially that God didn't create them that way. You did that by exposing them to negativity, foul language, and in households where they weren't taught anything but how to run wild. Loving the black child makes changes in our characters in order to provide them a correct chance at living a positive life. This is whether we had a positive life or not. That is no longer our concern. We have to look toward the future and do better by who we have brought into the world. The world is already evil and crazy. If we are the same we are just making our children worse.

Guide Your Man/Woman to You

Everyone has needs in a relationship that need to be met, but not all partners are used to having to meet those types of needs. New partners in new relationships need time to adjust to those needs. You are the only person who can guide your partner in the right direction toward loving you correctly.

You may have dealt with someone in your past that has spoiled you into being treated certain types of ways that your new partner isn't aware of. It is going to be your responsibility to communicate what you like and don't like to them in order to have a fulfilling relationship. Some people think that they don't have to say anything, and everything is just supposed to fall into place. The faster you make them aware of your needs, the faster you can be comfortable again.

You also have to be considerate of what your partner needs. Some women, for instance, are very sensitive; much more sensitive than others. They need you to take great care of their feelings. They can be so fragile that you can hurt them deeply by saying the smallest things that have offended them before. Men are not usually very sensitive and they have trouble dealing with emotional people that are too sensitive.

Some peoples' needs can be too extreme, but in order to learn how to deal with who you are with, you have to learn those needs as well if you want that in your life. You should always be up front about the amount of time you desire to spend with your mate, or the amount of time that you have to spend away from your mate. No two people seem to handle it the same. Women usually want more time, and men usually want less time; sometimes. You have to guide them on what you like and how you eat. If your mate doesn't cook, or know how to cook, you may need to show them. This will make you feel better to know that this person knows how to satisfy your hunger. You also will be teaching them something that they needed to know how to do anyway. Don't make them feel bad for what they don't do or don't know how to do. If you want them around you make them custom to you. Make them fit your needs and become everything to you. The problem that we face in society is that people are always hopping from person to person to get one or two different needs met, when the person they're with is fully capable of satisfying them the way that they need to be. If you don't let them know they will continue to just be the way that they've been. You can really turn a person off and ruin a good person, and relationship, by becoming angry and/or frustrated by what your partner does or doesn't do especially when you haven't taken the time to show them, teach them, or tell them what you do and don't like. It is nothing to be embarrassed of. It's more of a considerate thing. They want to please you and they need to know how. No one wants to feel like you are secretly disgusted by something they do or don't do. If you really want to be with this person it can only make it easier to customize them to you. You have to guide them to you. The worst case scenario is that they can't do what it is that you want or need them to do. But you'll feel better knowing that you informed them on what it takes.

Teenage Love

Feeling like you are in love with somebody as a teen can bring about real feelings of joy, ecstasy, and self worth. It is a high that most people have experienced in their youth and one that is quite unmatched and sometimes never happens again for people. Teenagers who've experienced teenage love get to somewhat experience what their love is made of, and how they may react and treat their future spouse. Except for one thing, they strongly think they will never have another mate for the rest of their lives. They believe that who they are currently with will be the person they marry and will love forever.

No one could tell me, still to this day, that what I had felt at that time wasn't love. It felt like true love. I've heard that it was just lust and that we were not going to last forever, and I could've punched them in the face for those words. But the truth was it wasn't going to last forever. We would have a pretty good run until we outgrow one another. Our young minds were not able to decide that we would never have desire for another person. All it would take is for one person to change and we would be history.

Teenage love feels better than adult love. There is neither person who has to worry about bills, housing, kids, or practically anything. You only take care of yourself to a certain extent. All you have to do is share common interests with someone else and grow to love everything about their abilities, their minds, their presence, and their desires. I believe that coming that close to the opposite sex, mentally, it makes the euphoria of lust get mistaken for love by both parties. This is especially true if the two are involved sexually. This is usually the very first time that you've experienced the opposite sex's attributes on this deep of a level. Physical sex further complicates the feeling by creating not only a need for the mind, but for the body as well. To an underdeveloped mind, the emotions related to sex with someone you truly care about is equivalent to the euphoria that a teenage underdeveloped mind has while experimenting with illegal drugs for the first time. It makes them want each other more and more every day. It is that much harder to go a day without them.

All good things come to an end though. Once the cherished feelings become a routine they stop feeling so good. Someone always winds up changing. The only problem is that when one person's feelings change, what happens to the other person's feelings? They stay the same as they always have been. Two hearts rarely break at the same time so one person seems to be fine. They can outgrow and move away from the relationship easily. The broken one is stuck with all of the so-called love in their heart. They find themselves not sleeping correctly, not eating, not caring, and wondering why. They never thought it would end and never wanted it to. Even if they were given an explanation they cannot grasp the fact that it is over. They are still addicted to that person. They cry uncontrollably and they beg and plead for second chances even if it was no fault of their own. This pain lasts for months, even years. My first love left me for unknown reasons, but I now believe her heart just left the relationship. It was no fault of mine or hers. It took me a solid two years to get over her. There were no discussions or negotiating about getting our relationship back on track. She was gone forever. Eleven years later, I still think about her all of the time. I never see her anywhere. I sometime catch myself feeling like I still love her and would drop anybody to be with her.

I say to all teenagers; spare yourselves this heartache. Learn to know the opposite sex as friends only. Don't try to be in love. It will hurt you later. No one really ends up being with their first love/high school sweethearts forever. It's just a phase that distracts you from family, friends, and school. Stay focused on school. You only have a few years to be young, then you will be grown forever. You can do all of that love stuff once you can handle the emotions. It is no joke being hurt when you don't even know who you fully are as a person yet. All you should be worried about is finishing school and being somebody. Focusing on someone else accidently takes your mind away from all of that.

What Responsible Adults Do

Too many people over the age of eighteen really have it stuck in their minds that they are grown. They think that just because they've reached a certain age that that confirms that they are now an adult. When in fact, most of them still behave like kids well into their twenties. They are still so dependent that they have no idea yet what responsible adults do.

1. Just because you have no one telling you what to do, that doesn't make you a responsible adult. Having self discipline, not running around wild, obeying the law, and allowing God and the right people to guide you in the right ways is what makes you a responsible adult.

2. Living with friends, family, and parents doesn't make you a responsible adult. Having your own home, learning to pay your own bills (because after childhood, you will have bills forever), and having your own assets is what makes you a responsible adult. This doesn't include those who've hit a difficult time at some point in their life and needed to move in with relatives in order to regroup.

3. Making babies doesn't make you a responsible adult. Raising them in a loving home with the hopes of them having both parents, making sure that they are well fed, taught well, and are properly educated is what makes you a responsible adult.

4. Being sexually immoral and jumping from partner to partner doesn't make you a responsible adult. Loving and being faithful to one person that you intend to grow with is what makes you a responsible adult.

5. Hustling in the streets doesn't make you a responsible adult. Obtaining steady employment, choosing to be around positive

crowds, setting goals for your future, furthering your education, and staying out of the way makes you a responsible adult.

6. Being an addict doesn't make you a responsible adult. Keeping your head clear, not putting yourself at risk of incarceration, not giving in to peer pressures, and not wasting your life away by chasing drug highs and intoxication from excessive drinking is what makes you a responsible adult.

7. Exposing children to bad behaviors, violence, gang members, abuses, and allowing them to view people and material depicting sexual natures doesn't make you a responsible adult. Keeping them shielded from harmful people and materials, and being cautious of your own behaviors around them; showing them that you respect them is what makes you a responsible adult.

8. Leaving mothers to be single parents doesn't make you a responsible adult. Sticking around; even if it's difficult, teaching your children, raising your children, watching them grow, showing and proving to your children and yourself that you are a great provider and father is what makes you a responsible adult.

9. Trying to be the hardest thug, the biggest gangsta, a big time killer, the 'baddest bitch,' or the quietest whore does not make you a responsible adult. Being career driven, educated, focused, having an entrepreneur's spirit, employed, family oriented, and a leader with freedom is what makes you a responsible adult.

10. Being a hater and blaming others doesn't make you a responsible adult. Worrying about yourself, learning what it takes to come up, taking responsibility for your own actions, paying your debts and dues, and keeping your word makes you a responsible adult.

Too many young people are running around thinking that they have it all figured out, when they really have no idea how silly they look and sound. There is too much drinking, too much smoking, too much partying, and too much poisoning. These things have them confused on what a truly responsible adult does. If you are the Y.O.L.O. type of person that does what you want and when you want just because you feel like you have all of this life to live, and you'll only get your act together when you reach a certain age, you're one of the reckless and irresponsible ones. If you know what you are doing wrong to yourself and your children and you continue with the behavior, you are one of the irresponsible ones. If you don't care how other people view your immoral activities, nor do you care how people treat you based off of those acts that you know are true about yourself, you guessed it, you're one of the irresponsible ones.

Dealing with Someone's Co-Parent

As loving parents and responsible adults we are no longer defined as 'baby daddies' and 'baby mamas.' Those terms describe deadbeats and runaways; male and female. We are parents and co-parents. And when you are involved with someone and they have children you are not only required to deal with the children, but you also have to deal with active co-parents in some kind of way.

First and foremost, the way this world has been ravaged by deadbeats and runaway donors you should take off your hat and salute any active mothers and fathers that you encounter. If you are dealing with someone with an active co-parent then you need to understand that this makes your life much easier. The load is taken off of you greatly, considering half of the time they are with mom, and the other half of the time they are with dad. Mother is usually less strapped for cash, so there is usually less that you have to worry about when it comes to her financial load. When children are enjoying their mother and father they tend to be smarter, more well-mannered, and happier. You don't have to step in and pull so much of the load. You won't have to be too much of a step mom or dad. Far less discipline is needed and situations that the children may encounter are easily handled between the mother and the father, who actually know and understand the children. The only job you have is to be there and take care of your mate and try to make their life easier and better.

Respect is the key to this kind of relationship. There are many factors that need to be considered when dealing with any kind of co-parent situation.

1. First, you have to know that any two parents must have effective and open communication if they are going to raise their kids right. This means that you have to give them that space and let them make decisions. Do it without interfering and catching attitudes. As long as the discussions remain about the kids, don't worry about anything. Don't even offer your two cents if nobody requested change. Just stay out of it.

2. Just because you heard this and that about the co-parent from your mate, don't attempt to judge them or treat them disrespectfully when you don't even know this person. You were nowhere around at the time and you had nothing to do with it. Don't confuse someone that is venting about their past or explaining what they've experienced as a reason for you to also talk badly and mistreat that person that you don't even know. What they did was what they did. You just focus on making his or her life better; if you can.

3. Never talk badly about a child's parent (especially in front of the child). This is the ultimate disrespect to a child and their parent. That child loves their parent more than life itself and can't defend their parent the way that they really want to. That child is also a reflection of that parent, so talking about the parent is like dissing the child.

4. Don't get in the way of visitation. Just because tempers have flared, or you just dislike the co-parent, that absolutely gives you no right to coerce the other parent to suspend visitations. Not only are you messing with the child's well being, you are causing further disruption and fueling an already heated situation.

5. Never pick arguments and fights with the co-parent. This just shows how immature and petty you are. You can't have much to do if this type of altercation is on your mind. Maybe you are worried that the co-parent did a better job at taking care of home than you. Or maybe you are more jealous at how they have picked up and moved on better than their ex did. Get uninvolved and get a life. Nothing makes a person look more miserable.

6. Be respectful at all times. If a person is only discussing their child, spending time with their child, and not bothering you and

picking at you then why would you get an attitude and be mad when they come around? If you want to make a co-parent feel some kind of way, then try being respectful and happy every time they see you. Try convincing their ex to be the same way. When you are always mad and disrespectful, the co-parent's ex tends to do the same and both of ya'll look miserable and stupid.

7. Never tell someone's kids to call you mom or dad. This is another ultimate disrespect. All that those kids need to do is respect you for who you are. Don't force them into calling you anything but your name. If later on they want to give you that title, then they will. Until then, try to earn it.

8. When you can, explain to the co-parent that you have no desire to mistreat or abuse their children. Let them know how much you care, and how happy you are when they are happy. At least give them that piece of mind since they don't know you, and you are probably around their children more than them.

The Young Black Father and the Young Black Child

This is a topic that is extremely sensitive and always has been very important to me. It is one that I will elaborate on many times, and in many ways. It is the need for the young black father to stay involved with the young black child. This doesn't necessarily have to be your own children either. But our children are being severely punished and severely damaged; becoming very lost and misguided. They are growing to destroy themselves by the absence of fathers, and father figures. This goes for the young boys and girls. Fathers really need to understand how large of an influence that we are in the lives of these children. The impact a father has on a child even a mother couldn't match it. We also need to stop giving these women the right to run around claiming and thinking that they could possibly imitate the role of a father in a child's life. A real father can explain how that scenario is no ways possible.

A father is ten feet tall to any child. We should take pride in being there to watch them grow before our very eyes. To watch them achieve academically. To be there to protect them. To answer all of their questions. To help them understand and see in you why they are the way they are, and how they think the ways that they think. How can a child that is lacking a parent fully understand who they really are as a person? They only know half of themselves. They need your encouragement, your humor, and your discipline. They need to see your face and believe in your word. Our daughters need you to be the first boyfriend/man in their lives. Your positive affect will be the reason that she won't fall off with the wrong boys that will use her for all of the wrong things. Your presence and involvement will be the reasons our sons won't fall off into the wrong crowds attracted to all of the wrong activities. If you were ever a boy that hung out with all of the wrong people, how many of ya'll in that group had a father around? If you've ever dealt with fast girls that started having sex early, had fast girl friends, and snuck boys in the house, how many of those girls had a father around? This world is already losing a lot of leadership and structure in the communities and it is a shame that our black households are growing up without fathers.

The women and mothers are not innocent in this either. It can be very difficult to be there for children when an angry, bitter mother doesn't want to allow it. I'm talking about a mother who is only thinking of her own satisfaction and not the best interest of the kids. They will be the ones that suffer though. The best thing that you, as a father, can do in that situation is to not play her games, don't argue, and be as calm at ALL TIMES as possible. She will eventually just be mad at herself. We must keep encouraging our kids that school and extra-curricular activities is all that they should be focused on. We don't need our kids worrying with adult situations, as it forces them to grow too fast. They tend to never slow down once that happens. We need to monitor what they are being influenced by in the world, and on television and music. They must learn rights and wrongs. They must learn consequences for their actions. Our own testimonies are great examples for them. Since children naturally follow in the same paths as their parents, certain things that we are trying to steer them from must constantly display roadblocks, caution signs, and stop signs. Don't just sit and watch as your children make the same mistakes as you did. They will do it easily, just out of curiosity sometimes, simply because they know that you did it.

If we don't stay actively involved as fathers in our kids' lives we will continue to lose them. As a real father, I don't see how one could not care about the well being of their child. We must care. We must first stop impregnating just anybody and focus on creating a real family. Black fathers are really lacking principles and standards and creating a lost generation of monsters. If you aren't going to do right by these children you do have the ability to run from them. But you won't run from the fact that soon they will never respect you. You will never be involved with your grandchildren, and they will find a way to break you down while explaining how you are a non-factor. Your life will never get right. No matter how good you think you're doing you will never find true happiness, inner freedom, or peace. Thank God for all the real fathers. God bless the involved fathers. Your children will reward you in so many ways.

Baby Mamas Using Kids as Weapons

I actually hate the terms 'baby mama' and 'baby daddy.' They both sound like degrading titles used freely, but representing a parent who is less than a true mother or father. It is a 'ghetto' term meaning that you are nothing but someone who merely gave birth to, or donated sperm for the creation of a baby. It means that you mean nothing else and they care about you even less. I would hate to be referred to as a 'baby daddy.' I am a father and my child's mother can refer to me as a 'co-parent.' Only time you are not a co-parent is when you are a 'baby mama/baby daddy' that is not looking out for the best interest of your child. A baby mama will use kids as weapons when they are this type of partner.

You can be with a woman for years. You can have children by them. They can swear up and down that they would never take your kids away from you if ya'll split up. The two of you can even watch several cases of women taking kids from their father. But why does as soon as the relationship ends, she turns around and does the exact opposite of what she said she would never do? She uses the kids against you. This is the oldest game ever. Once she realizes that she can't have you, or you've moved on to someone new, or she feels hurt or betrayed, she uses the only ties that she has to you against you. These are dumb, ignorant women. Even if she's the cause of the relationship failing, her own regrets turn into anger and bitterness when she sees that you have shifted your attention. Now she takes the one thing that she knows that you love and can't live without. She envisions them as twelve gauge shotguns and she turns them on you to kill you.

Newsflash to all sick, misguided, bitter souls. That blast will injure a father. There is no doubt about that. But the ones that you are killing are your own children. That's the one who suffers the deepest wounds. You would actually take a voiceless, helpless, innocent child and use them as a weapon? Then, turn around and tell the blind-eyed people that you are such a good mother and love your children so much. You are actually scum. Sooner than later the gun that you are using will turn on you and wound you. Nothing is destroying our society more than 'baby mamas' taking innocent children from their fathers because of their own bitterness and rage.

Another newsflash is that you won't come up like that. God sees you even if you are fooling everyone else. Once they are able to, those same kids will attack you in many ways while you are thinking that they are blind, deaf, dumb, and will be young forever. You will always be miserable. Until you do right by those children, everything that you try will fail. No child deserves a wretched, immature, simple-minded parent like that. I don't care why or how the relationship ended. Unless that man did something foul to those children, you couldn't give me a single excuse that I would buy. In fact, if you attempt to use the words 'I' or 'Me' in your explanation you have immediately lost me. It's not about 'you' or 'him' it's about 'them.' Ask yourself about rebellious children. Ask yourself about disrespectful teenagers. Ask about the ones that join the gangs. Ask about the ones that resent their mothers. This is what you are creating while you are cracking up laughing right now because your helpless child is younger than ten. You will be crying by the time they are sixteen though. When the weapons turn on you, you will throw your hands up and don't even know why they are acting out the way that they are.

You 'baby mamas' are destroying your own futures that you are supposed to be enjoying in your late 30's and 40's while you are only in your 20's. Trying to seek out revenge on someone by using other people to make the war is wrong. These episodes have lasting effects too. It is slowly creating societies little monsters and little devils that will pack prisons and destroy others because mama flew them through life without daddy. All of this happened because mama was hurt and decided to play a game. These are the pitiful women that love their own fathers to death though. They call on their own fathers daily but they deny their own child the right to call on their father.

Are You the Reason that You Became a Single Mother?

It's no secret that I don't believe that with all of this out of control, high rate of single mother homes that it is all the fault of the fathers. I speak out freely on the fact that more times than we know it all started with the rage and deviousness of a bitter mother. It's an old game with new players but the game is still played the same way. So recognizing the plays has never been easier. I ask the women are they the reason that they became a single mother?

Don't confuse it by thinking that I don't know that there are dads who've abused their children, who are not responsible enough or capable to handle their children, and there are ones who had no intentions on being around for the children. There are dads who even simply just walk out on the whole family for whatever reasons. There is a high rate of this ignorance. But that is not always the case. More times than you could think of a mother has initiated the problem causing our children to grow up in single parent homes.

Let's break it down. Women have long known that when the relationship ends they automatically gain control of the kids. That's the way that it will be when kids are made out of wedlock. Depending on her level of rage and anger toward the father, she calls the shots on how often and when she wants the children to interact with dad. You can notice that the more angry and bitter that she is, the more games that she will play. Face it, all women know that no court is going to take the kids from her if she isn't neglectful and harming them. No matter what the courts say about visitation, she will control that too. Should the father try to find her in contempt, courts usually side with the mother and no contempt is found and nothing changes. They laugh at the father because he is trying and failing. They brainwash the children into thinking that the father doesn't want them. They keep the children away for months, even years at a time. Some have even went to the far extent of letting a new boyfriend come in and control the visitation while he pretends to play daddy for whatever amount of time that he lasts. The mothers sits back and collect all the child support while denying the father and the child their rights. They do all of this because the justice system allows them to do it and she simply can. Judges side with the mother every time. This forces the father to run out of options. He is left tired, miserable, and he and the kids are helpless at this point. The police are not even allowed to enforce visitation and they will tell you they can't do anything but take reports on legal matters. All issues must be taken up with the same judge that is tired of seeing the two of you and doesn't really care about the well being of your child.

The truth is, mothers want to carry out their personal vendettas and eliminate the father from the kids' lives. They wind up running the father off. As she presses and presses him, he is left no option when even the court system isn't on his side. When a man can't find a solution he becomes angry and loses hope. In order to keep from winding up in jail for destroying somebody that chooses to play with his kids, it's in his best interest to just leave the situation alone. I mean what is he really left to do? Then years later when the kids get older and start becoming rebellious and harder to handle the mother needs the father back in the kids' lives. She caused him to miss out on so much. She caused him to grow apart from his children and now she needs him. Maybe it is because she has matured and realized how stupid she was. But all while the father was absent she convinced the world that he was a runaway; a deadbeat. She convinced the world that he didn't love his kids. All along, she silently played the game because she knew she would win. But she found out that she really didn't win in the end. Because of the absent father; the kids grew to hate school, they are disrespectful, pregnant at sixteen, sneaky, liars, gangsters, runaways, and juvenile delinquents. Their mother cries every night worrying about them. It turns out that God saw the games that the mother played over the years, and just like normal she had to reap the consequences for her actions. You may laugh in the beginning but you will cry in the end. Look out for the best interests of the child so that you all can enjoy life now and later. Doing it right makes life easier for everybody.

Being a Father; Dealing with a Spiteful Mother

The worst thing in the world that a father can have to experience besides the death of one of his children is a hateful co-parent. These types of situations are unbelievably tough because they involve the emotions and the well being of the kids. A bitter mother cares nothing about that fact though. She doesn't care about hurting an innocent, helpless child. She is focused on attacking a strong, grown man.

My family is a victim of this same situation and I had to find ways to be a father while dealing with a hateful mother. In the beginning I never thought that this person that I enjoyed raising children with would turn into the self-centered, cruel person that she'd become. She had no control over me ever, and when it was over I moved on, but she wanted revenge and control. She expressed her anger and hatred towards me, but she showed it even better. It was easy for her to pick arguments with me. It was easy for her to keep the children from me. It was easy for her to spend my child support money without allowing me and my child our rights. It was easy for her to turn her family and the court system against me. It was difficult for me to let her keep doing these things to me and our child. I thought only negative thoughts about her. I hoped for her demise. I just could never understand what mothers thought that they were gaining by keeping the children from their father. No matter what, when I seen her over the years she was still bitter and angry. She didn't look as healthy as she had looked during our time together. She was always miserable. She couldn't keep a home for more than a couple of months. She was crumbling right before my eyes. I could've laughed but I chose to always be bigger, stronger, and never be as petty as her or her family.

What must happen is that you first have to stop arguing with this person. In no way should they feel like they are getting the best of your time.

You have to learn to get to the point fast and easy, then hang up or walk away. She will want to argue, but never give her the satisfaction of getting under your skin. Learn to never get too personal about yourself or her. Don't even act like you care about what's going on in her life as long as it isn't hurting your child. Keep discussions only about the kids. Instead of being impolite, start being nice and never show weakness. If she won't bring your kids during your scheduled visitation, remain calm and nice and leave it alone. Document what has occurred, but never stop pursuing your visitation. Stay up on that. No matter what a judge says, keep filing contempt hearings. The judges talk like they are tired of seeing you, but this is what they are paid to do every day. These actions will mean something one day.

As long as you are seeing your kids never ever pick a fight. Keep her as calm as possible because you aren't concerned about the games that she's playing or what she is thinking any longer. You just want your kids when you are supposed to have them. Don't pay attention to any rumors. Stay firm, but not too aggressive about your child's well being and education. Keep your own tabs with the school. Don't seek out too much information from the mother. Whatever you can do on your own, do it. Her mission is to control you and bring you down. That is fine, and whatever, as long as you are seeing your children regularly. Make the kids all that matter and eventually she will see that she isn't getting the best of you. It takes a while, but the sooner that you change the game, the sooner she will follow suit.

Importantly, my point is that you NEVER FIGHT IGNORANCE WITH IGNORANCE. If you do you will see these games recurring for years to come. And eventually you will grow weary, the pressures will build up, and you will probably physically hurt the woman. That will never be a good situation for you or the child. Remember that the child loves you both equally and needs to stay out of all cross fires. Definitely don't talk bad about the mother in front of the child no matter how mad you are. Regardless, we still need these ignorant, immature, poor excuses for mothers to be well off, as that's the only way that we can be sure that our babies are well off when we aren't around.

Take Time To Teach Your Children

Get off of Facebook. Get out of the streets. Stop worrying about who's doing what and when. Get off of the phone. Stop chasing highs and getting drunk. Take more time to teach your children valuable things that they need to know.

It is not only the responsibility of the teachers at school to teach your children the basics about studies and life. These teachings must start at home. By the time your child has started kindergarten they should have started their ABC's and 123's. Young parents need to make sure that they are using what is being taught in school as a guide to what to stimulate when they get home. So if the teacher is currently teaching her class to pronounce ten different words, you should be at home doing the same thing with the child until they have mastered the words. We can't be getting so distracted that we forget that this is an everyday job that we at some point signed up for. Once the kids see you all distracted, they too will be distracted in and out of school. And the teachers can tell which parents are putting forth the effort at home.

Stop telling yourself that your child can't do something. This is only your excuse as to why you're not helping them. They definitely won't be able to do it if you constantly make them feel like they can't. Believe it or not, a child can do more than you think. It just takes more time, patience, and pressure. I had a three year old nephew that could show me how to find my own youtube channel on an Ipad. I have a daughter whom I made sure knew how to read fluently by the end of kindergarten. This was my determination as a parent. I also showed her simple ways of doing simple math that she is comfortable with and she is proud of

97

showing her dad that she can do it. I know that if they have all of that energy to run around in circles all day that they definitely have enough energy to learn whatever you take the time to teach them.

Besides school work, there are valuable things about life that must be taught as well. Like how to avoid strangers. Like how to not tell family business to other people and strangers. Like how to watch for cars when they are outside playing. Like how to dress themselves and tie their shoes. They need to know right and left. They need to know right and wrong. They need to know how to pray and why. Most young kids leave the house and don't even know their parents contact information, or how to dial 911 in case of an emergency. There is so much to teach these kids rather than just watching them grow up and barely know anything at all. You don't want them to have to learn from their friends in the streets. But they will get the game from somewhere. There will be hell to pay if you don't pay these kids attention and you stay distracted by what you have going on all of the time. When you made kids you took the oath to raise and teach them right. There will never be a day that they are alive that they will not need to learn something from you, even as adults. The more you teach them, the better off they are as teenagers and adults. You will reap the benefits by them staying out of trouble, being deserving of your trust, becoming responsible teens and adults, and prospering better in life. Untrained kids become unskilled adults that cause trouble and do ignorant things. They hate school, so they do poorly. They turn to the streets for help with what they don't understand, and most likely become misguided. When you see this happen, if you were the one that failed to pay them the attention that they needed, you can thank yourself. Now that their life has become harder, they will make yours harder too.

They Abused You, Don't Do The Same To Them

Not everyone had a positive upbringing with great parents and positive people around that stimulated educational growth and installed positive morals. More people than we know have suffered abuse in all kinds of forms and it's had a lasting impact on them well into adulthood. How the trauma of these neglects and abuses is released plays a big part in problems that we have in society today.

Besides the obvious extreme abuses like sexual abuse and physical abuse, many people grew up being abused mentally. They were told that they would never be anything. They were shown hatred and disrespect instead of love. They were misguided into thinking that the wrong things were actually the right things. Some people were just raised in a household and literally weren't taught anything. They were forced to feed themselves, forced to learn to clean themselves improperly, they didn't have to attend school regularly, and their sexuality was opened at very early ages. These things became damaging to the young person growing into adulthood, as they became more susceptible to evil people in the world that took advantage of their poorly developed mind. They were enticed to do crazy things and the women were impregnated with children at young ages.

Now that these children are here, born to people with rough upbringings and underdeveloped minds, they become the victims of the same life that the parent endured. Without really recognizing it, the person that suffered these neglects and abuses are exposing their children to the very same life. Men easily walk away or don't even care for the children well at all. Women seem to show the same characteristics that their abusers have shown them. Both seem to develop heavy drug and alcohol addictions; as well as sexual and party addictions. These types of traits affect the children greatly.

If you suffered this way as a child and you find yourself leaving your kids every weekend or throughout the week with other people, overindulging in alcohol/drugs, not paying attention to the needs of your children, cursing at or in front of them all of the time, not providing for them, looking out for yourself more than them, choosing mates over your children, and constantly taking out your anger on them, you are dishing out the same neglects and abuses that you suffered to your own children. You just may have a slightly different approach than what you experienced personally.

Most of us have experienced drug and alcohol abuse in our homes. We know about parents that are always switching mates, cursing heavy, arguing, and fighting. These things were mentally unhealthy and should not be acted upon in front of your children if you don't want it to have the effect on them as it obviously had on you. We can get caught up in not knowing what is affecting a child because they aren't effectively expressing their feelings, but what they see and hear, whether you know it or not, it has a lasting effect on them. The same way that it did with you. Let's do better by our children because they will grow up someday and bring all of that back on you. They will tell you about yourself eventually, as you may have later approached your abuser as well. Allowing young kids and teens to drink and/or smoke weed and cigarettes has never been, nor will it ever be cool. Their underdeveloped brains do not need the stress. Shame on you if you are providing your children with the same life that you grew to understand was wrong.

When They're Not My Kids

In this land of the single and free it's not going to be difficult to run into the guys and the gals with kids that don't belong to you. This will prove to be very challenging when you have never been in this situation before. Whether you already have your own children or have no children, dealing with someone else's kids is totally different. It's going to take a lot of patience and understanding when you decide to take it on. But if you really want to be with this person you have to accept their children.

Assuming that we talking about mothers and fathers that are involved in their kids' lives, dealing with fathers is different than dealing with mothers, whom are usually the custodial parents that has the kids all of the time. If there is no father around, this makes the situation much more different. The kids are most likely always going to be around the house, the mother has it harder when dealing with them, and there are more expenses to deal with that the mother is taking on by herself. These things have to be taken into consideration first.

1. *Always inquire about what parenthood is like for the mother.* Hopefully, she isn't one that hollers that she has bad kids. That may just mean that she's a bad mother and the kids are probably worse than you think. You are good if she says that they are smart and well mannered. Some kids that grow up without a father lack these skills.
2. *Don't ever think that it's a bright idea to move into a house with strange kids that you haven't had the chance to get to know well.*

If you are impatient you may find things that they do that are very irritating to you. You may have made this huge life change just to later realize that you can't handle it.

3. *Let mother know about any wrongdoings and/or disrespect, but never ever ever attempt to physically discipline someone else's child.* This could cause major problems between you, mom, and the biological father. Give yourself the chance to see how effective the mother is at disciplining her children.

4. *Interact with the kids.* They are going to be there so you might as well learn what they like and dislike.

5. *If you are having a hard time adjusting, discuss your concerns with the mother.* This is better than holding them in and walking around with an attitude.

6. *If you see the mother lacking somewhere and it makes you uncomfortable, voice your concerns to her.* It may just be something that she didn't know, but something that she can change.

7. *Know that the mother has possibly been used to raising her children a certain way by herself and she too needs some adjusting in order to fit someone else into the picture.* Be sensitive to this situation. Mothers love their children and they discipline them the way that they do so it's hard for you to be aggressive in this matter.

8. *Teach the kids new tips and tricks that will allow them to grow into you and learn to like you for who you are.* They don't know you like that either and they want to learn you as well.

9. *Don't ever talk bad about their father, whether he is there or not.* This is equivalent to talking bad about the kids. They are a reflection of him.

10. *If you find yourself disliking the situation; leave it.* You can't take the mother away from her kids because they aren't going anywhere. So you are the one that has to go. It sucks that you couldn't get to her before they did, but it is what it is.

11. *If you aren't ready to be involved with someone's children; then just stay a friend.*

12. *Let the kids see that you respect their father and their mother.*

13. *Love them and tolerate them as you do your own children, if you have any.*
14. *One of the best things you can do is make their mother's life better and easier.* If they've experienced their share of downs, the kids would really appreciate seeing their mother come up. Because when she comes up, they come up. It will get you plenty of respect. As a matter of fact, it will get you all of the respect that you initially felt like you deserved but didn't earn yet.
15. *Don't talk about the kids.* Kids are innocent. Whatever you feel that they are doing wrong that falls back on the parent. Don't dislike them or treat them badly.

It's the same rules when it comes to dealing with fathers. Take extra precaution with fathers, as they have very limited time with their kids. So naturally they want to give them the world in a short amount of time, so you just may lose a little bit of attention on the weekends or something. Just know that any good parent is sensitive when it comes to their children and their parenting. Whatever you feel about them they will pick up on it quickly. So stay away from treating peoples children differently or acting differently when the children come around. You will never win and take the place of the kids no matter what. They aren't going anywhere. All you can do is be there to help or just remain a good friend. As long as they aren't disrespectful and ill-mannered it shouldn't be too hard to adjust. You just have to go into the situation knowing fully who the children are and what they are about. Learn what areas may need some help and understand if you do or don't want to get involved. You have to have the right attitude and patience. Nine times out of ten it's the adults that need to do the most adjusting in this situation and nothing will go right until the adults are right. Kids adjust to love and affection easily.

Dealing With a Sick Child

The hardest, most unexpected experience to have to deal with is when you have to deal with a sick child. Being confused and barely knowing the questions to ask, or what to do, would make one weary and afraid of the outcomes that they may have to face. It is definitely a scary time when you have someone that you love and care about at risk of having long-term complications, or even facing death.

My first child passed away to heart disease one month before she could turn one. The experience in hospitals and being at home with her sent my parenting level into overdrive just like it was supposed to do. Having a sick child is nothing to play with. When the doctors tell you that your child has an illness be ready to learn everything that you can about the problem. Learn it inside and out, using all off the resources available to you. This is the time when you have the chance to sympathize with and understand the way that your child may be feeling. Do not sit around and wait on the doctors to tell you everything. Instead, show them how much you know. This was something that I didn't do initially, but once things started to get serious I got serious with it. I should've been serious from the very beginning though. You don't want to be uninformed about the condition during any stages of it. What you learn can later help your child and the doctors. Doctors will be impressed by how much you are involved and they will feel comfortable sharing more with you; as they know that you are ready and able to handle more technical information. It won't be easy for them to withhold anything from you if you are already on top of your game.

If and when your child has to take medications, stay on top of that and be sure to give the right dosage at the right times. Be very aware of what you are giving them. Study the medicine like you would study the condition. And be sure to give it on time, all of the time. Do not slip on this part. It is easy to make matters worse if you become irresponsible and think that it is alright to miss or give late dosages. Doctors can't tell if you are at home doing what you are supposed to do, so if something like this happens, they won't know why. Learn the side effects and the way that this medication is supposed to treat your child. Pay attention to how they react to the medication. People react differently to medicines so stay up on it.

Any questions or concerns that you have don't think twice about calling the doctor. Your child depends on you. Doctors care a great deal for your child, but they have many patients to deal with at once. You have just one to focus on. Anything that you need to know, you need to ask. When you have ideas, express them. I used to do my own research and find different methods and medicines that the doctors could possibly use to help treat my child. I expressed these to them, and sometimes they used them, and sometimes they didn't. They all were taken into consideration though. Doctors aren't perfect and they can use advice and opinions from involved parents that care.

You also have to know that you don't have to sit and wait on the doctors to call the shots. You are actually the shot caller for the child. You approve and disapprove treatments for a reason. They ask you to sign for every procedure for a reason. It is your call if you want them to do what they proposing or not. Take advantage of being involved and in the decision-making by participating in the doctor's everyday discussions if your child is being hospitalized. They will let you sit in these meetings involving your child. Ask questions about why they want to do certain things and have a clear understanding of what they are saying and what is going to take place with your child. Never feel pressured or rushed into anything if it isn't already critical. Call the doctors into your own meetings when you have to, and write down all of your questions that you want to have answered, beforehand.

Overall, your child's health and recovery depends largely on you taking good care of business. Knowing the problem, working with doctors, giving medications on time, and being sensitive to the condition and needs of your child will help for sure. You can't guarantee anything, or play like you are God, but you can do the best that you can to make sure that your mind is at ease knowing that your child is well taken care of.

Think About the Future

I have a young daughter. I hope to one day be blessed enough and have set myself up enough to send her out into the world with some valuable tools that will ensure that she won't have to struggle with the things that I struggled to get and maintain. I want her to already have a house and a car. I want to have all of these things all paid for. I think about these for her future. I don't want to just raise her up and send her out into the world. I don't want to just send her out to the wolves. I want to be able ease the major struggles for her.

It's very important that we teach more than we preach. Not only for our own children, but for all of the youth that are looking up to us. Show them at early ages the value of home ownership and saving their money. This way, even if you are able to provide it, they still know how to appreciate it. They will understand why they shouldn't take these things for granted. Let them know about evictions and how you could be on the streets by not paying the rent, and how many times you were stressed about finding and maintaining shelter. If no one tells them these things, they won't know until they bust their heads wide open going through it. The teenagers need to know, especially. They need to know what more it is to owning a car than just driving it. Nobody takes the time to really drill these things into the kids minds, so it's just preaching and no teaching.

I remember there wasn't much emphasis on college and being certified to do professional things in my home. And by the time that I was a junior in high school, I already had my mind made up that I wasn't going to anybody's college. I saw no reason to. Nobody in my family went at the time, so I followed suit. Now I wish that I could've been certified at something by the age of twenty-two instead of trying to figure out something to be at thirty.

 So much that could make life easier needs to be installed in kids and teens and young adults. Kids are too busy running around in circles all day, teens are too busy trying to fit in on every level, and young adults get on their own and start busting their heads on everything that they attempt to do. They haven't been trained right and taught to prepare themselves for their near and distant future. They are just simply raised up and sent out into the wild. The youth need to fully understand why they don't need to be in a rush to be grown. Don't give up on them and just say, "You'll see." This is a natural setup for failure. Youth need so much attention and so many examples to see and feel. They need less preaching and more teaching.

I wish that I would have cared about my future. I wish I would have seen someone else who cared about their future. I wish someone would have guided me on what I was going to later on learn and possibly take a bruise from. This includes employment, shelter, and the law. The law was one of those things that I should've never gotten mixed up in. I did hear about getting in trouble and you go to jail. But why should I have ever been scared of jail? And really, I've grown to not be afraid of jail. I'm terrified of what happens after you get out of jail. And that is if you get out of jail. You have to deal with lawyers, the court system, probations, and alternative sentencing. All of that stuff is no joke. So don't just talk about the basics with these kids. Explain it all in detail.

This is why I'm glad that I did experience all that I did. I will have an in depth knowledge and insight to give to my child, and the youth, on a variety of topics. I am definitely not going to hold back from her the information that I think that she should know, and that I know that she will understand. From teenage sex and pregnancy, to education, to politics, to current events, to adult concerns. I want her to be fully knowledgeable so that she doesn't have any excuse to make the mistakes that myself and other people have made. I want to put aside money, a house, a car, and an education fund for her to get a good push. I want her to know that she will make mistakes but she won't just run into wall after wall because she has a lack of knowledge.

Teach them all that you can now. Prepare them for the future. Let them know what can make or break them because you too were broken by similar things. Teach them now because you won't know when your time on earth is up. I'm not scared for mine to grow up better than I was. In fact, I encourage it. I want them too. I know that they will be extraordinary people then. I could never be so selfish to want to wait and watch my babies bump their heads. I'm not the one that is excited about intervening and saying, "I told you so." Whether I'm here or gone, I want to know that mine are educated, gamed-up, strong, and ready for the world.

Dreams: Do You Take the Stairs or the Elevator?

Dreams are a part of life that makes it interesting and worth living. The majority of us have dreams that take us to new levels and ways of thinking that we have never experienced. They are God given missions that are personally gifted to us to make something of ourselves and create a better life for our families. So naturally there is a goal to reach. The question is, "do you take the stairs or the elevator when trying to reach your goals?"

What I have learned about having dreams is that they aren't made up of one goal. They are made up of many goals that you constantly have to setup to accomplish one mission. I've been working hard at my dream for the last five years and can't seem to find the finish line. I now realize that if I do happen to get to a finish line I would have more ideas and more goals involving the same mission that having a finish line is more like a checkpoint instead of the actual finish. There doesn't seem to be an end and that's what makes it all the more better. Since life keeps going on I'd rather hit checkpoints instead of finish lines. It keeps my mission going and interesting. The more accomplishments you achieve, the more recognitions you receive for your hard work; as well as being prouder of yourself to the point where you feel like you can do so much more. And you will too.

Also, what I've found is you have to be patient when chasing dreams. Be careful not to set timeframes for reaching a finish line. Instead, set time frames for reaching goals. Goals are easier to reach when chasing dreams than it is to reach the end. Don't rush to the end and become frustrated when you don't get the results you desired. While you are living a life that is separate from your mission you can't expect life to stop for your dream. When you get too caught up in rushing your results, discouragement sets in and it makes it too easy to quit. You should realize first and foremost that when you are on that race track moving towards goals and checkpoints that there are sights you must see and things that you must learn along the way. There are people along the way that help you get from goal to goal, checkpoint to checkpoint. We started with nothing but an idea and must realize that all of these things along the way are to help us grow and learn what we are actually doing. They show us what to do and what not to do. They show us who to deal with and who not to deal with. Hard work and consistent efforts must be applied to get things accomplished. The more that you run toward it, not necessarily the faster, the more you learn about what you're doing. Checkpoint to checkpoint you bump your head less and less. You get from here to there much swifter, thus, reaching your accomplishments faster. The more that you slack, the more you get set back.

Without speeding through checkpoints you gain valuable information, resources, network connections, and knowledge than you would by skipping levels. This is what I mean when I ask, "do you take the stairs or the elevator?" People who take the stairs move more slowly, more cautiously learn everything that there is to know and they tend to save more money depending on what it is that they're involved in. Those who take the elevator speed through checkpoints taking less precautions, learning less, paying everyone to do everything for them, and they take a greater risk at failure. It's not impossible for elevator riders to get there because the idea is to get there faster. The problem is that when they do get there do they have enough capital and knowledge to stay there? Without the knowledge you still have to pay everybody so that you can use their brains.

I hated that my mission wasn't where I felt that it should be in five years. But I now realize why it takes time. I realized that while I'm accomplishing goals and keeping it alive I still needed to be changing myself with it so that I can fit it. I can't front though, in that time, I've learned nearly every skill necessary for my dream that I needed to allow me independence in all of my projects. Things that I've dreamed of knowing I now had the desire to learn how to do them. And I did just that. These are the things that keep me on the stairs, and they also keep the dream alive. Knowledge became power that would be valuable to me even if I were to stop today. What I've experienced and learned will never be forgotten, nor can I ever regret the time and money that I'd invested. It turns into a winning situation either way.

Stimulating Your Great Mind

Having a great mind can also mean having a curious, overworked mind as well. Great minds never sleep and they constantly form new ideas and thirst for new ventures. New goals for current missions require much stimulation from sources outside of the mind and it is important to surround yourself with people, places, and conditions that will have a positive contribution to your objectives.

The company we surround ourselves with can have either a positive or negative effect on how you stay motivated on your ideas. Positive people will encourage you to do more and they will listen to your goals. They will give you the necessary input that you need so that you are not only working and executing off of one brain. Positive people tend to be more helpful and they allow your mind to be at ease when making difficult decisions. They understand better, while caring more about your progress and achievements. Whatever makes you happy makes them happy too.

Negative people around you will cloud your mind with too many judgments and negative thoughts. They can make you start to feel indifferent and you won't even know why you feel that way. You have to stay away from these types of people. They only want to see you doing bad or doing nothing at all. Usually they have nothing going for themselves. The only reason they found their way into your situation is because they just had to be nosy. They heard too many good things and/or your name circulating with such good news associated with it that they had to see this for themselves. These are the distractive people. They will never say anything good, or sometimes say anything at all when you let them in on what you have going on. Negative people stimulate your mind in ways that make you change your mind for the worse, or just flat out give up.

The type of places that you visit can have a good or bad impact on your mind as well. For instance, trying to live a healthy, alcohol free life but you steadily frequent your favorite bars, that can have a negative effect on your progress. But hanging out in the church, or with family members who keep good spirits, can have a positive effect. Things that take place in these places tempt you to do one thing or another, and it's usually what others that frequent those places are doing. You want to frequent places that will keep your mind focused on the objective, not where your mind will be pulled away from it.

The conditions that you surround yourself in mean a lot too. As a writer, I find it hard to write where there is too much noise or there are people who will distract me. These conditions make me lose my inspiration quickly if I wasn't already prepared to tune it out. When you are somewhere without the right tools it won't allow you to get the job done. Working in a dirty kitchen won't even allow me to cook right.

Certain things just need to be considered when stimulating your mind to allow it to grow and get to the next level. If you aren't in the right situations it can send your mind into a backspin and cause you to fall off. You can come with all of the right intentions, and also exit out leaving all of the wrong impressions after doing all of the wrong things; accidently. It's too easy to get caught up in thinking negatively when you are surrounded by negative people. You can allow yourself to get used to lower standards when dealing with unsatisfactory conditions. You should give your great mind the proper stimulation that it needs, as you would give your car the correct amount of fuel to get you where you need to go. The adverse effect that the wrong people, places, and conditions can have on a great mind can really destroy a great thing in a great person. Sometimes you have to plan ahead and let yourself know what will and what won't work for your situation and really stick to it.

Use Your Time Wisely

What's just as worse as someone who is unmotivated and lazy is the person who thinks that they have all of the time in the world. I mean really. That just isn't true. Once that person actually starts to do something with their life they will actually realize that there isn't much time in a day at all. Considering household/family business, work, and other various obstacles that life brings you will learn how important it is to use your time wisely.

Just like anyone on their mission can tell you, it is always the smartest idea to plan by the day or by the week. This will give you specific goals to follow instead of scattering everything in your mind and becoming overwhelmed and frustrated. Planning helps put things in order of importance. The brightest minds have the tendency to race faster than the body can keep up with, sometimes leaving you thinking of goals that aren't due until further off in the future. This is still good because it keeps you prepared to tackle your next moves. They just need to be captured and planned accordingly, by either writing them down or copying them to a computer. Either way, you still don't want to miss out on beneficial ideas because they do come rapidly.

When you find yourself in between jobs this is the best time to make something that has been pressing on your mind come to life. Some people have had ideas that they couldn't launch off because of working long hours or they just couldn't find the motivation, the drive, and/or the time to get it off the ground while they were working. This is the best time to put it all together. Financing usually turns out to be the problem though, along with worrying about how the bills are going to get paid. But this is when planning becomes helpful. Also, instead of sitting around and moping more than you are doing actual thinking and planning, use the down-time to get started at least. Most ideas have the ability to get started without investing money anyway so this is the time that you can use to get the business part of it in order. Learn what expenses you will actually have and take note of what it's going to take to get going. The talented part of it is the easy part for you, and since that is free, you can get going on that part right away. When in between jobs you have more time for research and you are able to do better networking. Spend more time in the library. It will put you around all of the proper study material and get you out of the house, where it is usually more difficult to stay focused.

All of the time in the world is at your disposal when you have nothing to do. Even if you are not working, you will find that once you get started on your mission that you will still not find enough time in a day. While you are applying for employment and waiting on return calls, it will be very beneficial to get these important steps going. Because when you do start working again you will already be off the ground and running. This will allow you to have a mind that is at ease with what you are doing on the side while you are at work. It is nothing like going to work and knowing that once you get off you will be working on your own project that you put together already. This is great when your dream is to someday stop working for others to enjoy your own home-based business, store, or music business etc. You could really get a lot done if you use your time wisely instead of staying down and out.

Using time wisely involves more scenarios though. I've given incarcerated people advice on writing books and reading books that will further educate them while they're down. I've done the same with people who can't work at all. I've convinced people that just because the body is down that does not mean that the mind is not working hard still. We are put here to be hard workers at something, but never put here to become a waste of space. One of the smartest, most innovative men in the world is paralyzed from the neck down. He lives in a wheelchair. It saddens me to see so many young and middle aged men and women who just give up on life and the possibilities. We see them all of the time. They live off of assistance. They would rather rob and steal. They would rather talk bad about others who are trying to do something with their life. They just roam through life as the beasts of the earth do without creating any kind of future for themselves or their family. At least if you don't succeed everyone could at least see that you tried to do something. You could always live with the fact that you did try. If you don't waste time doors that you never thought would possibly open for you will open up.

Don't Discourage Me

Never will you go into anything with all of the praises and joy from those around you. Nor will everybody you come in contact with have your best interest in mind. Not everyone will want to see you succeed. Many people will act like they do. They may say that they do, but truthfully, they don't want you to, or could care less if you do.

Watch out for these types of people while you are chasing your dreams. These people are one of the poisons that can drag a person and their dreams to the ground. This is not to be confused with those that offer criticisms and/or feedback. You need certain criticisms. It helps you reevaluate and make beneficial changes that you probably weren't aware of until it was pointed out to you. It's not easy, nor recommended that you make all of the final thoughts and decisions based off of your one brain. But don't let discouraging people anywhere near your thought process.

Discouraging people are the ones that could really care less. They hear your excitement and see your enthusiasm and they turn a blind eye and wear deaf ears. They usually have nothing going on for themselves so they don't care about what you have going on. They are quick to change the subject on you. They make you wonder why you even asked them or told them anything. They clearly don't care.

Other discouraging people are the ones that smile in your face, but you hear about them or can sense that they are the ones that are talking behind your back. These types of people mostly come from your own network. These are the ones that see you do what you do, and when you think they are proud of you and rooting for you, you find out that it was the opposite all along. Somewhere it went sour. Maybe it was something that you said or done. Maybe there is some jealousy or envy that kicked in. Some salt was shaken somewhere. Yet they still smile in your face because they want to see how long you will last. In their snake eyes they see you destroying yourself or maybe they plan to destroy you.

Lazy and unmotivated people discourage by not caring and not having anything positive to say. They are quick to respond negatively to whatever you say or think. If you needed their assistance they couldn't wait to say NO. They laugh at you when something fails or falls apart. Don't argue about anything with these types of people. They will say the most hurtful things that will stick to your mind for a long time. They sometimes apologize for what they said and say that they didn't mean it, but the truth is what they said is what they really feel and mean. They are out to discourage you because they hate the level of excitement, confidence, and enthusiasm that you have. They have none of that for anything in their life. They envy your bright mind, and trust that they will say more mean things to you when they get the chance.

Stay away from these people. They will turn your mind and ideas upside down if you let them. It's not always easy to rid yourself of these particular souls because they are usually trusted associates, family, or network contacts. But anyone that doesn't have your best interest in mind will definitely be preying on your downfall. You surround yourself with enough of these people and you won't think straight at all. Your visions and ideas will take a turn for the worse and you will find yourself trying to figure out what it will take to please the naysayers, when this was nowhere near the plan in the beginning. The best way to deal with discouraging friends and family is to not include them in anything that has to do with what you are doing with your project. Don't discuss anything. Keep them wherever ya'll were before there was ever a mission to begin with. When they inquire let them know that you are doing fine and change the subject. You don't need negative looks and feedback to interfere with your thought process. It changes too much and it hurts too much. Don't even allow it the opportunity to go there. When it comes to network contacts, shop for different ones. There is always more than one person for the job. Network contacts come and go anyway. They only have a season in your mission and when they start to acting flaky it's time for them to go. Keep only positive people that can stimulate your mind positively around you.

Take the Best Route

Once you understand that there is a lot of things out here that one can get involved in, but can't do, you will be able to narrow down what it is that you're supposed to be doing. Don't confuse it, we can do whatever we want to do, but everything isn't for you. This is when paying attention to God, your past, your skills, and what you are passionate about comes into play.

We have free will to pursue whatever it is that we desire. But have you ever tried to pursue something that you are just only curious about? How long did that last for you? Have you ever noticed that what you are naturally passionate about or have gained a skill at is usually the route that you wind up sticking with? It is because it works for you and we are going to find comfort in what works for us. Things that we are just curious about, we gain knowledge of that particular life, we get our fun and kicks out of it, but it winds up somehow blowing away or endangering or getting us into trouble sometime. It is something like the curious person that has witnessed the flamboyant life of a drug dealer. They think that they can do it the same way, deal themselves a hand, play the game, turn around and lose badly in the end. They didn't have anywhere near the good run or get to be as flamboyant as the person that sparked their curiosity.

Skills are skills though. You will learn many skills along the way and it is good to pick up as many as you can, when you can. Different skills help you pick out which one you enjoy the most and would like to make a career out of. These help you distinguish which places of

121

employment to apply to also. It's always best to apply only to places that match your skills unless there is something that you are very interested in learning how to do. This saves you time and money, since this is what employers look for when choosing the right candidates for the job. Your skills are what define you. You can currently be working in a factory, but if you've been a cook for the previous eight years, you will always consider yourself a cook because of your many years of skill in that area.

Taking the best route can promise a brighter future for you and your family, but that all depends on you. When you find yourself steadily changing, it makes your life go up and down. You will know what works and what doesn't work for you. This is when you apply one of the other skills that you possess. But trying to do what the next person is doing isn't going to always benefit you. That is what was intended for them to be doing. This is why our passions are different from person to person to begin with. Trying to be like the next person will not get you the same results. Even though we may have matching interests, God's plan for us is different than those that we are compatible with still. You may both be interested in food, but one may just be interested in eating food, while the other really enjoys handling food. It sounds the same when both people say, "We like food." But one is a cook, and the other is a customer.

Think about the road that you are trying to take and concentrate on that road more than what other people are doing in front of you. You must understand some are meant to do this and that or make more or less money than you. But what they're doing and how much money they're making means nothing if they aren't content with what they're doing to make the money. People do get caught up and get stuck doing things that they don't wind up enjoying because they let what someone else is doing appeal to them more than sticking to their own route.

Keep You on Your Mind

We can easily spend our time worrying and caring about everybody else and what they have going on. We can obsess about our children. We worry about what our family and friends are doing. We are just worried about everything instead of focusing on ourselves. Then we tend to let important information and opportunities pass by us. We stay on the same levels when we don't keep ourselves on our mind, first.

Learn to help yourself first before you rush out to jump into everyone else's situation. Some people are blind leading the blind, and struggling leading the strugglers. Then when the receiver gets on their feet, they start to talk about you because they have figured out that you were and are worse off than them. There is nothing wrong with getting things right on your home-front, beforehand. People see this and they become inspired to do better for themselves. They become more willing to listen. It gives them a platform to see and follow. They rarely listen to someone who is doing just as bad as them. They just use them as a stepping stone that they don't even appreciate later on because of what they have seen them going through.

You can't let everyone live in your house for free if you are barely keeping the bills paid. They will eventually raise the bill so high that the services will get disconnected. You can't let everyone drive your car that already needs many repairs. They will tear it up even more and then you will be left stranded. When you can't afford to be brought down, you can't be afraid to say NO. We all want to help and be a blessing, but you can't be that in all ways, every time. This doesn't take the care out of your heart at all. It makes you more concerned and responsible for you.

When people need help that you aren't in the position to provide, don't worry, there are other people that they can ask. If it wasn't you that was around, they would seek the help and find it somewhere else regardless. People can also take advantage of someone whom they think is vulnerable, or gullible enough.

Don't miss out on opportunities or visions that God is presenting you either because you are so worried about what you can and can't do at the time. When you think of all the things that you can do, understand that you found the time and energy to do those things somehow. Some people let kids and spouses dictate how they move about their lives and accomplish things for themselves. They are sadly causing themselves to lose out. Kids are supposed to be raised correctly. They will soon be grown enough to go off and do their own thing. You don't want to be stuck where you are now because you only cared for them. Your spouse is supposed to help you move along. But spouses don't always last forever. If they go off and do their own thing, then only caring about their needs and wants over the years will have you stuck right where you are. It's better to get started on something for yourself; something that you can count on to move you along even when no one is there. You don't want to be in the position where you have passed up on so much over the years that now you live with all kinds of regret. When God gives you a vision then act on it. You never know what obstacles or mountains He will move, or move over, in order to allow the plan through. You won't know either if you just disregard everything.

There is always something out there to achieve. There is always ways of bettering ourselves. Save yourself and it will become easier to please and serve others. Learn how you 'do you.' Take this into account, "who is going to save you when you are all dried out?" Keeping you on your mind keeps you determined to live and to grow. You will have less tolerance for nonsense. People won't run to you to use you for your resources all of the time. You won't even let them. When you have everything to share and to give, you learn a valuable lesson once you wind up with nothing. It's like feeding the birds. They won't show any appreciation, but will return everyday at the same time, with the same appetite. You are the one left with the empty loaf of bread. If you don't have money for another loaf, then you won't be eating any bread that day. They fly away to start their day on a full stomach. God indeed blesses you for all of the generous deeds though. So, you will eventually get another loaf, but all you will wind up doing with it is worrying about all the little birds that depend on you to feed them day after day. Being generous and helpful is great and highly recommended. But make sure that you can afford two or three loaves sometimes. You need one for the birds; and plenty for yourself. Don't always go out of your way for others and cause yourself to crumble.

Built to Last

I can't explain enough how important it is to remain tough and strong through all of the pressures that we encounter on this earth. Or how important it is to not give up or give in. It is equally important to pay attention to the signs and the examples that we see all of the time. A lot of these slips and fumbles are the same slip ups that we've seen and heard thousands of others make. Therefore, a lot of this stuff we have no excuse to be so naive about.

The person that has had ups and downs, and learned to be a responsible adult even though is what I like to call a person that is 'built to last.' Being 'built to last' is the one that has learned from their mistakes and the mistakes of others. They just chose not to become another statistic. The person that is 'built to last' won't need God to allow them to bump their head over and over to get them to learn. They will see what won't work for them and switch it up to please God and make their life improve. A person that is 'built to last' is in no way the follower type. They notice that followers fall over like dominoes; one after the other. The 'built to last' person has to stand strong and tall at all times. This person is also a role model. People have seen this person go through hardships but always bounce back or come back stronger than before.

The person that is 'built to last' is very impressive. People enjoy being in their presence and hearing what they have to say. They love to be a part of the moves that he/she makes. Being built to last, you have to be big and strong. You don't show any weaknesses. Everybody expects that you have strength on all levels at all times. They rarely think a person that is 'built to last' has regular feelings and emotions. So you have to keep those in control as well; as people will never treat you like they would treat a weaker person. God gives the person who is 'built to last' many blessings, but many challenges as well. This is what makes them stronger. It also gives them much testimony. People will envy this persons great strength and endurance. They will want to be the same way when faced with difficulties and will remember what they've learned.

The follower is never 'built to last.' The ignorant are not 'built to last.' The ones that purposely set bad examples are not 'built to last.' They run in and out of jails and prisons. They never experience having their own assets. They prey on others weaknesses. They crumble as soon as they are put under pressure. They have no strength. They have no skills. Instead of being an achiever they take life threatening risks. They don't care about their life or your life. Anything they've ever had they lose it as fast as they received it.

When you are not under pressure to be in with the 'in' crowd and you are content with being who you are and serving God's purpose, you are setting yourself up to be hard as steel. God creates His people everlasting so that nothing can break them. Worries don't actually make you worry and problems aren't really problems. Everything that you need to conquer any situation will be given to you without you having to go to extremities to get it. If you can't pay a bill or pay to fix the car, the person that is 'built to last' will trust that God will deliver. And He will in some kind of way; and right on time. You won't need to panic and think that you must run out and rob or steal or sell some kind of drug. Your mind and your faith wouldn't allow you to be so weak. The only way that you can be 'built to last' is if God has made you that way. The people that you think are the toughest and the most flamboyant, are the ones that are the weakest and that vanish every day. We lose them all of the time. It just looks like that to you because they live a lifestyle that you don't. The ones that are really out here surviving, paying their bills, walking straight paths, taking care of their homes like real providers, and enjoying freedom day after day and year after year are the real, everlasting people. Others may have their season with all of the easy money and lavish-looking lifestyles, but what happens to them when they are pulled off of the streets? They become dependent on the very same ones that they looked at as peasants. They depend on the ones that they laughed at and said that they would never be like. It's now about the ones that they previously hurt and let down. They depend on the ones that are 'built to last.' Even though it may not look like much to today's big time players; when they do fall off, at least you still remain present and strong. So who is built tougher than whom now?

Having Faith in the Hood

No matter where you are from, if you know how to keep faith that God will keep you safe and protected and make it possible for you to come up in life you have the right mindset. Many things can go on around you but you don't have to fall victim to any of it. Staying prayed up and trusting God is the key to making your life better. Hard work makes progress and gets you several steps closer to being who you need to be and going where you're supposed to go.

No one has to be stuck in poverty stricken communities or trapped dealing drugs for the rest of their lives. Keeping faith and communication with God, and trusting Him, will take you to levels that you and your peers never thought were possible because of where you all are from and the conditions that surrounded it. When you think of other young people in the hood you don't hear much about them praying or fellowshipping about God. You hear some mention coming up, but you hear and see all of the worse ways that they plan to make that happen. You rarely see any of them actively seeking a job. You rarely see any motivation or drive to even want to work. They don't want to do anything positive for that matter. It's just a bunch of followers and a bunch of gossipers. So who, besides maybe the elderly, is trusting that God will keep them safe and provide for them if they were to fight the pressures to do wrong; but instead do the right things?

There is nothing wrong with doing the opposite of what everyone else is doing; especially when you see people poisoning themselves, losing their families, and dying over the same things that everyone is hyping up as the 'right things' to do. Why do we feel so pressured to do these same things still? These outcomes for these actions are no accident. This type of lifestyle was set up to fail in these ways. It makes no sense for us to still fall into the same traps. If no one is praying and trusting God, but people are dying every day, wouldn't you think that God's route is the better route over everyone taking their own routes?

If drug dealing is landing every dealer in jail, or eventually prison, isn't it a better idea to seek another legitimate way to make money? People who believe in and trust God live different lives than those who only believe in themselves. The ones that only believe in themselves easily fall victim to evil and wicked people and things around them much faster than those that are protected by God. You will be amazed at how different you see things that are glorified in the hood after you accept God into your life. A lot of the things that people say and think and do will sound and look so ignorant and you will pray even harder that God guides you swiftly and quickly to the nearest exit. And He most definitely will.

A lot of the times people want to make these changes and these exits but they haven't made the changes to their thinking and/or ways. They still get tied up into the same situations with the same people. Man isn't strong enough all of the time to make these mental changes that will shift their minds to solid exit strategies. When you want your life to change you have to change with it. God is the way and the beginning to making that change. If you just depend on you, you will find yourself constantly falling back into what you're used to doing. God shows you the alternative paths and how to get there. Before you know it, your old friends will have nothing to do with you anymore. Your old ways will vanish and no longer look appealing. Your old thoughts will make you ashamed that you even had them at one point in your life. God has no problem proving to you that He is real if you just have faith and continue to trust Him. Don't go back on your word and be pressured by those around you. When devils test you, keep being strong and don't go backward. Try to do the opposite of every negative influence around you. They will have nothing to do with you after a while and that is fine and the way that it is supposed to be. When they don't know how to handle you anymore and start appearing to be envious you will know you are on the right track.

Power of Networking

Being able to network is one of those skills that gets us to the next level in what it is that we are striving for. Like they say, "it's not about what you know it's who you know." This proves to be true in so many ways. You can have several degrees in the medical field, but if all that you network with is fast food managers, all that you will get is referrals to fast food joints.

Networking is essential in anything that you are striving for. This is why I say, "when you are chasing dreams, don't take the elevator." When you move too fast from level to level you miss out on important networking contacts along the way that could be very beneficial to the future of what you're doing. This is a big no-no. It puts you at risk of having to do much more than what you would've had to do. Networking with other people doing similar things as you allows you to touch bases with people who specialize in other areas as you. For instance, you may be a video editor, but the more people in video that you network with, you may find newer and better software, and people who shoot videos that you can edit for.

When you team up with these people you can take your business to another level by being able to provide more and/or better services than you could before. One person is capable of doing a lot, but the more you are willing to network, the more you and other people can help each other. Networking should never be left out of any business moves. Visiting business people at local meetings and networking with people on the internet can open your eyes and ears to more ideas and possibilities that you didn't even know existed. Listening in on open conversations amongst others and asking questions will get you in the know. Good networking can open the doors overnight in some cases. Most are just as excited as the next at working with the other. Each individual has something unique and/or different to offer as far as the different styles and brainpower that they can add to the equation.

You can also network good enough to find investors for your projects. An excited person automatically tries to figure out how they can front the expense for projects on their own. Getting around the right people you can find that like-minded people with money are more interested in funding the project for you. You have to be willing to get yourself in front of these people though. They are everywhere and this is a part of handling business. I think about all of the live rap shows that I've done that never would've gotten done if I had not gotten out there and networked with different promoters. Not only did they book 85-90% of my history of live shows earlier in my career, they were the cause of my music and name taking off on the local level the way that it did. It all seemed to work together. And if I wasn't in the building on the day that I was, expressing my interest in the ways that I did, I would've missed out on opportunities that changed everything for me.

Networking is a nonstop process. Along the way you are going to want to meet and mingle with everybody that can give you that next bump up. Everyone won't prove to be all for your come-up either. It may start off looking and sounding good but it could turn out to be disastrous if you see they are out to take your money or they are only trying to benefit themselves. This is why you should keep looking out for beneficial people that you can grow your team with. You will know when you have a good team in place and everyone is eating correctly. Until then, don't put off networking with good, like-minded people. Always look to share with others your tips and tricks to help them along the way in their journeys; whether ya'll are a match or not. Don't be afraid that others are interested in stealing from you. Everyone is trying to help everyone succeed. Besides, learning from you doesn't at all mean that they can do it just like you. Good networking involves helping one another. Most likely, you learned quite a bit from other people too. This is one of those times when it's handy and helpful to talk to strangers.

Giving and Helping

Giving and helping is like borrowing a blessing. Just like you don't ask for the blessings and they seem to just come; it's the same way when you give to someone or help someone. They didn't ask for it, but you blessed them anyway. You don't ask for anything in return and neither does God when He rewards you for your good deed.

Giving to someone in need, or the less fortunate, always makes one feel good. It also looks great in the eyes of God. We should always have the spirit of giving. You know when it's the right time to give when your heart is pressed on making something happen for someone who is in need. Everyone isn't able all of the time, including us, and what you are able to do will become a blessing to someone else. Not seeking anything in return is the smartest way to give. Otherwise, it just turns into borrowing. Although both are kind gestures, one should look at the benefit of less worry that the receiver would have rather than adding on debt to them. When one gives, they can be sure that God will bless them for their generosity time and time again. People in need find themselves deep in prayer, in distress, worrying, scared about being able to pay bills and provide for their children, and in many stressful situations to the point where they are unsure where to turn. And when God presses it on you to be the blessing, understand that He also made it possible for you to help. You were chosen to come in His place, and as a part of His plan you were appointed to save that person. It's the same when you are in need. Sometimes the greed in us wants to expect something back in return. But would you be more satisfied with your mere investment back or would you rather wait on many gifts and blessings from God?

It is pretty much the same with helping someone. When you need help people run to your rescue depending on how much you have been willing to help someone else in need of your assistance. Some people hardly ever find anyone who seems to want to, or are available to help them. But these people also fail to realize how much they are unwilling to help others. Naturally, life won't stop for them when they need help. It is up to that person to learn that they really do run away from helping other people. God acknowledges this as well. He doesn't let anything get to be too much for His people, so they will get what they need, but it will be a bittersweet experience getting them to understand that they will need help one day also; just like the person that needed their assistance. Simple help shouldn't be overlooked. Simple help brings about great blessings that are as large as helping someone in a complicated situation. It is all about where your heart is at. Dropping what you're doing to help an elderly woman carry her bags, or pulling over to give a person with a dead battery a jump may be small business to you but it is huge at the time to the person who needed the help. If you are wandering around the area and able to help, it is much better than that person waiting an hour or more for someone to come and help them. This can inconvenience them by having them stop what they're doing, find the tools, and go out of their way. Small things count and people are very grateful to you for it.

Making it apart of your normal big-hearted practice to give to and help others will keep you receiving multitudes of blessings and gifts over and over. This is how you make it through life comfortably. You do it by helping and giving. If you ever wondered why people jump to help you out, or if you wonder why God blesses you so much, this is part of the reason why. You must have a good heart with a strong desire to be there for His people. It's rare to not have what you need for you and your family when you are always willing to help others. It has nothing to do with being rich or poor, nor happy or sad. Poor people can be the largest blessings in others lives. They are the ones that know what it is to be in need and they know what joy it brings to receive help when they need it. So their hearts are usually the kindest anyway.

Those that stay away from bragging about what they've done will receive the reward. It does not need to be publicized what you have done to help someone. Keep it between you, the receiver, and God. Everyone will know how much you bless others by seeing how blessed your life is all of the time. As stated before, we are only able to give by the grace of God anyway. Without Him wanting you to or allowing you the ability to, you wouldn't be able to give anyway. So be thankful that you are able to even be a blessing to someone.

Love for Your Neighbor

Just because a person doesn't look like you, talk like you, or think like you doesn't mean that they aren't a good person. It's time that we start looking at the good in people instead of judging outside appearances. Everybody wasn't made to be the same, but that doesn't mean that they couldn't possibly have the same things in common as you, or could help to benefit you in some kind of way if you were to stop and acknowledge the person that they truly are.

The friendliest person is the one with all of the connections. They stop here and there to chit-chat with different people, and not being shy gets them gains that they would have never had if they hadn't approached the right situation. This is how you get job connections, side hustles, new partners, and network connections. Showing strange people that you aren't stuck up or snobby makes them feel comfortable sharing with you.

This is what it's all about. It's about having love for your neighbors. This could be someone that you are in class with, in the grocery store with, meeting at a common place, or just about anywhere. Random people have things going on in their lives that you might find very beneficial if you happen to get involved. They will never know your interest if you treat them like they don't exist. Small talk can turn into plans and business moves before you know it. You never know who God is putting into your path, and why. Have you ever noticed that when you are in a public place and there is some strange person who somehow seems to catch your attention? You may bet that if you exchanged a few words with this person that it would be an interesting conversation. You may even sense that you and that person could possibly have something in common. Look at the place where you are meeting this person at in the first place. It is a mutual spot. The reason that each is there has to be somewhat on the same level as well. You can share ideas about where you are, and possibly get answers to questions that you may have had.

Also, people that you don't know, but you've heard about before, can be interesting to get to know. Now you can be clear on what you've heard about them. If it was something that you always wanted to be a part of, now you may have a chance. It is cool to get rid of all of the wonder and get down to the facts.

Finally getting to know people on the opposite ends of life than you are on can open the doors to many possibilities. It also draws you away from the comfort zone of always dealing with the same kind of people that you are used to. This is not a bad thing for a lot of people either. We need to get away from old ways and ideas at some point in life. This is especially if it hasn't gotten us anywhere. Having love for people and being able to enjoy people makes people want to be around you and to help you. There are so many times that I've stood around just chatting with a complete stranger and left with new outlooks and new visions. The benefit does not really ever involve me having to interact with this person any more than the time it took to be enlightened by them. You have to understand that people love to share knowledge and information when they know that they can help, and when they know someone needs it. All it takes is a simple inquiry sometimes. When God gives you the words to present to the servant, take the blessing. You will pass it up over and over by being anti-social and only caring about you and yours. I've walked away from talking with people and thought to myself, "That person had to be an angel in disguise." It just seems that we met in the right place and at the right time.

Keep your eyes and ears open to those that are trying to get to know you. They may be able to help you, or you may be able to help them. People that are sitting around talking loudly like they're having an open discussion can spill valuable information and resources that will benefit you too. Don't get too distracted and annoyed. Sometime you might just want to pay attention. They may just spill what you need to know.

Today's Young Black Leader

Being a leader is like being a positive role model. The leader is someone that all people can admire, and that the youth can look up to. Even without a large following, people that come into the path of a leader will automatically take note of your attributes. Either they are with you, or against you. The leader has respect from people for who they are and what they do. Nothing that anyone says or does will steer them from what they believe in or what they consider to be the truth.

1. *Today's leader will have love for people.* You won't find a hating bone in their body. They are more concerned with inspiring and helping anybody. They want all people to succeed and do well, but they understand the fact that everybody doesn't have the same love for others, and everyone doesn't have the goal to do well or succeed.
2. *Today's leader will stay positive.* Negative ways and negative people make them sick in a way. But the sounds and sights of their words and ways is the main reason that they feel the need to stay positive. They realize the world won't change its negative ways if everyone follows the negativity and forgets what the right ways are.
3. *Today's leader helps others.* They thrive off of seeing people get and achieve what they need. They also realize that the more people that they help, the more blessings will come their way as a reward. Helping others is a high to them and they know how contagious it could be.

4. *Today's leader will share their testimonies.* Usually, someone that has the qualities to become a great leader has seen it, done it, and survived it all. Sharing testimonies inspires, educates, and teaches others. People learn from someone who has knowledge and experience much better. A person who has a testimony to give understands that you shouldn't neglect your own past while you are teaching others how to have a better future.

5. *Today's leader thinks differently than most.* While others get caught up in the hype of jumping on the bandwagon, the leader sticks to what makes his/herself happy; while being careful not to think and do things that will make them take foolish losses. They stay away from ignorant thinking that people express publicly and they refrain from judging people about their thoughts and words, since untrained minds are naturally attracted to ignorance.

6. *Today's leader will lead by example.* They know that even when they least expect it people are watching. The leader is careful to practice what they preach. They know that going down the wrong paths will make their words and their walk less appealing to those looking up to them and eventually it will mean nothing at all. The leader cares deeply about the way that he/she is viewed by the public. They know the level that they want their admirers to get on is the same level that they are on, or actively striving to get too.

7. *Today's leader stays away from stereotypes that have defined the black culture for years.* They will achieve this by not being on the bad side of the law, the police, and the community. They will stay positive and helpful. They will love and not hate. They will build instead of break. The stereotypes that involve the way that we talk, wear our clothes, hang out all night getting into mischief, and more won't define today's leader.

8. *Today's leader will stay away from drama.* In fact, they will promote peace by being peaceful when drama approaches them. They will also encourage others to do the same. The leader won't be drawn to the nearest fight that is drawing a crowd. They won't be a part of the post-fight discussions. Drama in any kind

of form, whether in homes or the streets will not be appealing unless it includes coming up with a solution to a problem.

9. *Today's leader will stay away from abusing drugs and alcohol.* The leader sees the destruction that it causes our people on a regular basis. The leader speaks and thinks with a clear mind, and encourages others to follow suit. If the leader has a history of abusing drugs and/or alcohol, he/she knows that by eliminating that part of their life becomes contagious to those around them. The leader knows that starting with self, there will be more people who give up their addictions and the better the community will start to become.

10. *Today's leader will get involved in volunteer events throughout the community.* They do this not only to help, but to meet and greet with the people in the community, other leaders, and politicians. The leader sees this as a way to be a blessing, and a platform to getting known and starting their own events; while having public recognition and backing. The leader will attend community meetings to learn about what's happening around the public on a local and state level. This is in order to relay the information to those that are following him/her since they don't inform themselves regularly.

Never a Hater; Being An Inspiration to Others

The only time that you should want to and the only thing you should want to hate is when you don't have the answers and/or the solutions to your own issues/misfortunes and you are not blaming anyone else but yourself. You should hate when you don't have the correct answers for someone who needs your input/advice. You should hate it when someone else needs help, and for some reason you can't find a way to help them. These are the things that you should hate. You shouldn't hate someone else for what they have or have going on that you don't. When you see someone at a low point in their life, you shouldn't look down on them or ridicule them. If you are going to do anything for them, be an inspiration.

I believe there are three types of people. There are haters. There are people who are inspirations to others. And there are people who just don't care about others at all. Haters never really seem to have much going on for them self anyway. They just breeze through life. They meet a bunch of different people, befriend them, then become jealous and envious of what they have or have going on. They plot, they scheme, and they take from those people. Whatever it is (family, money, attention, shelter, job, a life, etc) that they have, and the hater doesn't have, the hater can't stand it with a passion. They laugh in that person's face, but talk strongly behind their back. I have learned the way to get them off of you immediately is to throw it in their face what it is that you do. And when they start to hate on it, then that is when you let them know that you know what they hate about you. They will get on the defensive and vanish from your life in seconds. And never will they return because their envy and hatred overrides anything that they can respect about you.

People who just don't care are easier to deal with, but they don't necessarily make good friends to have. Maybe they are cool associates, but take them lightly. These are the people who don't have time to hate because they have their own things that they are focused on. They are pretty insensitive to others' situations. Talking to them is like talking to a brick wall when you are discussing your personal issues. When discussing a business issue, it better involve them in order for them to care about it one bit. Like I say, these are people that you can just be cool with for months, or maybe even years. They are your social partners. They don't care to be around your family or your problems. They probably would most likely like to keep you out of theirs as well. They don't mean you any harm and never dig into your business with the hopes of misguiding, misleading, or talking about it behind your back. If anything they will have an ulterior motive behind their desire to know something in particular.

The ones that are an inspiration remain an inspiration through and though. No matter if they're up, down, high, or low. These are the people that know the value of support, teaching, advice, and strengthening others. They know that people who call upon them are confident that they won't be misled by them. They are excited to share their knowledge on specific topics and to share their supreme thinking power to help others grow at whatever they're doing. An inspirational person has needed help at some point in their life and they have been blessed before. They pay blessings forward by blessing others. They trust that God sent helpless people to them for the blessing. He gives the inspirational person the words to speak and/or the good deed assignment. The receiver listens, absorbs, and acts on what was delivered. This is the high that an inspirational person feeds on; as they feel that this is how they receive the bulk of their blessings. An inspirational person can never want to be a hater. They are too obsessed with helping others. They don't care that the next person has more or less. They are more determined to help them gain more on either end. An inspirational person is more disturbed by those that seek help and guidance with no intention on acting on the newfound wisdom. I'm talking about the people that listen closely and agree, but return to their normal way of thinking or doing as if they haven't absorbed a thing. It is very hard for an inspirational person to keep a secret on how to get something done when they are sure that they are about to help, heal, or strengthen someone. They know that if that person were to apply the right methods they will become successful at what they are doing.

Poison for the Body and the Mind

Too many things are cool that are not really healthy at all. Too many people are popularizing the evil and the worst things around that will destroy us physically and mentally. For some reason we have not learned the importance of keeping our temple clean and our minds clear. Different poisons for the body and the mind stay entering us and our youth. We are destroying ourselves and don't even seem to care enough to recognize it.

Drugs, alcohol, and tobacco are probably always going to be the most common poisons that take us over. These three things have been our biggest killers ever. More and more kids and adults are inviting these killers into their temples. These killers poison our minds by allowing us to change personalities while under the influence. They flip our moods up and down like a light switch. They have caused us to pack the jails and the prisons; banning us from having our freedoms. We find ourselves chasing drugs. What kind of sense does that make? Our minds become so poisoned that we follow the leader, and the leader is the drug. Our minds have become weak to addictions and our bodies suffer diseases and failures because of it. Yet, we don't seem to pay any attention, or even care.

Surrounding ourselves with negative people has poisoned the minds and bodies as well. It's too easy to be pressured to do all of the wrong things with negative people. They assist us in helping our minds stay hooked on drug addictions, and expose us to other negative things including: sexual immorality, violence, negative thinking, hatred, and evil ways.

Our minds and bodies are poisoned when we give in to these acts and behaviors. We can find ourselves changing who we are as people without us even recognizing it at first. Even the people that we are partnered up with can be poison to us; especially if they are blatantly exposing us to diseases, lies, deceitful ways, and putting our lives in danger.

The things we watch on television and on the internet, hear come out of other peoples' mouths, and the conditions in which we dwell in can be very poisonous as well. These things need to be monitored and regulated thoroughly. This is especially when it has anything to do with our children. When poisons get into our bodies we not only become a risk to ourselves, we become a risk to those around us. Drugs, tobacco, and alcohol have poisoned people to the extent that they become disillusioned to how they are losing their families, their jobs, and their lives. They are so poisoned that they keep doing it so that they don't even have to care about the possibility of losing everything that they have. Before it comes to killing ourselves, there is a chance that we will wake up in jail cells being charged with crimes and have to realize now how we are poisoning ourselves. The violence and sexual depictions on media stations have people thinking all of these things are normal, but we are losing people to death and jail cells every day because of it. The people that give us drugs and hype up violence offer us the same fate if we allow them to poison us.

You have to be smart enough to keep these things out of your system. You have to control what you allow your eyes to see. The same must be regulated for your children. Once the poisons have entered your temple it is hard to shake the thoughts and feelings away. These poisons are highly addictive, and if they weren't they wouldn't be absorbed and abused by so many people. One of the reasons why this world and this society is so obsessed with negativity and addictions is because many people are poisoned. They indulge in poisoning their minds and bodies. Since they are already poisoned they convince other people that it's alright for them to do the same. Misery loves the company and a lie doesn't care who tells it. Keep your temple clean and pure and resist these poisons that have a fraction of the population stuck. They aren't going anywhere but down. They also look silly while they are doing it.

Violence amongst Each Other

I know that we are living in an evil world and we live amongst animals, but are we the ones that are creating the beasts? We are bought up hard nowadays and made to think that we are supposed to be tough, but could this be the root of the problem concerning the increases in violence amongst one another?

Violence is going to exist in some forms, but while we prepare ourselves to protect ourselves, we are also preparing ourselves to attack one another. At any time I can find myself in a group of three to four guys under the age of thirty and hear about every robbery and every murder that recently took place in the city. If you want to know about the underworld of your city then all that you have to do is stand with the 'lords of the underworld.' The ones that were built to be hard and tote weapons and start problems in the community. They may not have done a thing, or wasn't involved in any kind of way, but they know all of the details.

These are the ones that are promoting the violent behavior that is going around. A lot of people like to blame it on the rap music but that is small compared to the groups of young people who stand around all day conversing about who did this shooting, who committed this murder, and who robbed who. I can't stand these discussions because the same people only talk about the same thing all of the time. They know nothing positive that goes on, but they know about everything bad that happens, and when it happened. You don't find these types of people in the library learning something. They aren't in school. They aren't in the church. You can find them in everyone's cars and in everyone's faces gossiping about foolish stuff that uninvolved, civilized people have no clue about. They know too much about the underworld of the city and they walk around carrying guns and hiding out from their own enemies that are actively looking out for them.

They talk money, mack, and murder all day everyday because this is what they glamorize. They glamorize murders, robberies, and other forms of violence; and they idolize people who commit such acts. They also commit these acts. They leave bystanders and listeners on the edge wondering if they need to be worried about such and such that they have been informed is going on, or if they should be arming themselves when being in certain places. Violence is hyped up and actively recruiting new offenders and victims. Being an innocent bystander, standing around a bunch of talk of violence, makes ones forget that as long as you don't get yourself involved with these people that are talking about it and committing these acts you don't have to worry about any of it. All of this talk about who such and such doesn't like, what they will do when they catch so and so slipping, who the next victim of whatever violent act will be is very ignorant, nonsense talk that keeps our brothers and sisters dying every day. If you aren't involved in these things don't wind up in these senseless conversations that promote death upon our people. The underworld will be the underworld and the game will remain the same. Let them play the dangerous games alone. Don't get all hyped up by what they are hyping up. It's the hype of the evil and the wicked. They will always kill each other over money, mack, and drugs. This is why violence will never end. The wicked will kill the other wicked all of the time. The innocent and righteous that are in the presence and the paths of the wicked tend to get knocked down too. Stay away from violent-minded, wicked people.

If we continue to hype them up, engage in their stories, live amongst them, represent what they represent, talk how they talk, and believe what they believe, hide them out, support and supply them, and love and encourage their behaviors; we are the ones that are creating the beasts and the animals of the city. When they start getting the righteous people on their side then we are responsible too. We can't keep feeding them and feeding their egos. It's like allowing the evil and the wicked the opportunity to dance and play around in our loving homes and churches. Let's stop encouraging this behavior. And maybe they will want to start behaving like us. Righteous people have been interested in, attracted to, and supporting the evil ways and people of the world for too long now.

Avoiding Beefs and Altercations

Beefs and physical altercations seem to be the result of dealing with too many people; or people whose levels are offset from yours. People that disagree with you all of a sudden want to beef. People with jealousy and envy for you all of a sudden want to beef. Bullies and people that prey on the weak will find anything to beef about. When they know that you are a peaceful person, people what to start trouble with you.

First thing is first; stay away from people that aren't on the same levels as you. If you do everything, and they do nothing, the opposites will collide. Jealousy and envy builds up and they either want to try to take you or take from you. This is going to cause you to react. It can start out as a simple argument that leads to an all out war. Do not be a motivated person that keeps the company of unmotivated people that have nothing to do. Starting problems is all that they want to do and they will try anything to keep you from coming up if they feel like they can't join you.

You also have people that just love to fight. Ignorant people that a pop off anywhere and at any time. Stay away from these types. Nobody knows the root of these peoples' problems. They were obviously raised wrong and in bad environments and conditions. They maybe were abused as kids. You know this type of person if you've ever encountered someone that you have a disagreement with, a few words were exchanged, and the next thing you know they are all in your face making threats. As long as they don't attempt to put their hands on you, end it right there. Nothing else needs to be said or done. Once you fight with ignorant people, then you wind up realizing how pointless it was and hopefully you didn't get into any trouble for these fools. If you have to pop off on somebody at least the drama should be for more than a disagreement. The best thing for bullies and people that just have to be so hard is to not accompany them at all. Don't participate in their discussions, laugh at their jokes, or have anything to do with them. They prey on you and pick you out by watching how you move and the things that you say. The less you interact with them or around them, the better chance you have of staying under their radar. If they interact with you and they sense a weakness they will try to trap you and test you. They don't bother the ones that they don't know anything about though.

Most often, beefs and physical altercations result from differences amongst friends and family. It's usually the ones that you know the most, and the ones that know you. Avoid these as much as possible. Everyone has disagreements; but some people are so sick in the head that they can't have a legitimate argument that will result in a solution. The only way they know how to handle problems is with violence. When friends fight chances are high that they will never be friends again. If they do, the relationship will never be same. During heated arguments, they already know so much about one another that the hurtful words go back and forth, piercing the hearts of each other. This pain lasts and hurts very bad depending on what was said or how it was said. The relationship can be destroyed just off of the words alone. It's the same with family. Family members fight and go many years without speaking. This angers and frustrates other members of the family. It separates kids from family members. Sometimes these separations are over the smallest disagreements. But, the intensity of the situation and the depth of the hurtful words said can outweigh the initial problem all together.

When you avoid these beefs and physical altercations, friendships are allowed to mend easier and faster. When one person is the bigger person and shuts it down, the drama will end sooner. No one will sit around and argue with themselves for too long. And if they are mad they'll eventually get over it. You just have to make sure that your words aren't taken too far to the point where physical fighting occurs. Someone who is trying to draw you into a fight, for whatever reasons, will try to convince you and others that you are being a punk; but backing down when you haven't been struck or attacked is simply being the bigger, smarter person. Later on, the aggressor will feel stupid for their actions. They hate that they ever tried to provoke you to create a situation that could have caused them to lose somebody over something so minor. You, being the bigger person, actually made it easier to forgive and forget. You can move on without having any devastating memories that will forever put a strain on any kind of future dealings with this person. Another thing to remember is that some people handle altercations with a level head, and others only know how to handle altercations with violence. Which one is the smarter choice to you?

Avoiding Peer Pressure

Avoiding peer pressures is not just for teenagers. It is the same for adults as well. With the number of rebellious hot-headed teenagers and impaired-minded adults these days, it is far too easy to get caught up in what the next person is hyping up. Peer pressure has been the cause of too many people dying and going to prison, but it is ways that it can be avoided.

Peer pressure is the reason I made the biggest mistake of my life, which was smoking weed at a young age. At the age of thirteen I knew that it wasn't right and that my mother never would have approved of it, but I did it anyway. Seventeen years later it has been the reason that I tolerated nothing but low-life friends, received a criminal record, lost my mother's trust, destroyed my high grade point average, and lost my desire to better my life by doing something with myself. In fact, I was so young when I got started that I don't ever remember having much of a desire for a better life. I never gave much thought to what that would consist of for me. Pressures to join gangs, pressures to have sex, and pressures to live like a thug consumed my teenage years ever since and made me more vulnerable to peer pressure as an adult.

Since the types of friends and habits never changed; neither did my way of thinking ever change much. So what I was likely to give into as a teen, I gave into the same things as an adult. Now as an adult with my own independence and no one to tell me what to do, things had gotten better for me. But it was all for the worse. I may need to explain that a little though.

Now that my mom wasn't telling me what type of friends to have, she also wasn't there to control that either. That may seem good except for the fact that now I just let anybody in the house that I wanted. I tried and thought that I could trust every one. These same people lied to me, stole from me, got me caught up in their messes, tore up my house, ate up my food, plotted on my girlfriend, my girlfriend even plotted on my homies. They manipulated my mind by making me think that their drug dealing ways and fast lives and money were the right way to live. Also, the ways that they used and abused women were glamorized. No one worked, no one had positive goals. Everybody was a gangsta. My poor eyes watched and my body followed with no one to tell me no.

Drugs were a part of the equation way too much. Mama wasn't there to stop me or cuss me out now. But, indulging in drugs too much landed me in weird places around very strange people. They also landed me in jail a number of times. It was also easier to experiment with other drugs besides weed. Alcohol and cigarettes were also used in extreme amounts. If I had any sign of a good life before, that was fading away fast. Now I had become a walking zombie. Mama would never have allowed this, nor would she have ever been proud of this behavior.

The girls came and went. They were only there for drugs, alcohol, partying, and sex. If there wasn't so much pressure to get as many girls as I can and have sex with them all, I never would have thought to put myself at risk of so much heartache, diseases, blowing money, and spending time on all of these different personalities that never wound up being there for me when I needed them most.

When considering being like the 'in' crowd, or your best friend, or a family member consider what the downfalls will be for you in the long run. The most notable peer pressures have the most long-lasting consequences. Everything looks and seems cool, but the only thing that is cool for you is what you have thought up on your own and doesn't involve harming yourself just because someone else is harming their self; and doesn't mind watching you do the same. A teenager's mind is not developed enough to make such decisions that puts them and their bodies at risk of disease and danger. I don't care how smart they think that they are. I used to be one of the smartest. A young adult's mind is usually tainted and diseased by decisions that they made as a teenager and they find themselves struggling to get ahead in life after that. I am one of them. Not many people were smarter and made better grades than me in my schools either. Nor have many young adults that surrounded me had more jobs, cars, and cribs than me. If you don't make good grades or consider yourself to be smart, you definitely need to be careful on how you poison your mind. Thinking wrong poisons the mind as much as drugs and alcohol. Don't give in to peer pressures that aren't positive and don't have your best interest in mind. You will surely live to regret it. This is no matter how cool it looks to you.

Dealing Drugs in America

I am no stranger to dealing drugs. I have never been the man at it, or a kingpin. It actually was never anything that I felt that I had to do anyway. I did it for the experience (skill) and the fast money more than anything. I sold crack cocaine once in my life, and marijuana maybe six or seven different times throughout the years. I was never arrested for dealing drugs, but it definitely came with its set of downfalls and prices to pay. I never got to live as fast as I wanted to, but I did get a taste of the life.

I hear how it is pumped up and glorified in rap music, but the experience can be very bittersweet. Truth is, drugs can sell themselves. You don't have to have very many brains to sell drugs. This is why even dummies love to deal dope instead of getting a job where you might have to use your brain.

The life is what it is portrayed to be in music and movies too. Overnight, you can have the money. You will have the girls. You will have the attention. All of that is a fact. That is not to say that you will know how to keep the money, the girls, and the attention though. People fall off just as fast as they get started by not knowing what they're doing and understanding the game. Everyone loves the dopeman that can stay on though. You will find your day to day surrounded by addicts that have befriended you because you went from a scrub to a thug. You went from bummy to flashin' money. It will start to feel like you're the man and that this is the life. You might even be able to take some of the miles off your shoes and put miles on a new car.

Now for the kick in, just in case you thought that that's all to it, wait till this kicks in. Every dopeboy falls for the attention from the ladies. These thrill seekers and gold diggers will lie around you and suck your profit dry. You will find that the longer that they're around, the more that they are going to want money for all kinds of nonsense. They need to be fed all day and they definitely don't want to try your cooking. They need drugs and alcohol all day, and you need them also just to be able to deal with all of the leeching that is going on. They want your time, which takes away from the hustle (money). And when you attempt to stop providing these things, or if you fall off, they are on to the next best. When the reality is that they didn't care about you anyway. Girls love attention and money. They were trained this way. They don't love you at all. In fact, the two of you didn't love one another. But everybody isn't tough and some of you are tender enough to fall for some of these girls.

The money goes as fast as it comes. So never think that you will just have piles of money. It's called fast money. You make it fast, you spend it fast. Dealers hardly ever know where their money went. You see them with a stack today and broke tomorrow. If you see a dealer with a pile of money you can bet that all that he is doing is flashing. It really isn't play-play money. The bulk of this money goes to the dealer's dealer. If he loses his mind and play-play with it, he just fell off at that moment right before your very eyes.

Dealers are at an everyday risk to snakes, cops, and robbers. The more they see you with, the more they prepare themselves to come take from you. This is dangerous living and leads to death and murder charges. These outcomes are never certain. People that you know very well will case your house and burglarize it, or they will just flat out rob you. And trust me, it's always somebody that you know and deal with that has gotten envious of your dark success. They're the only ones that know you, your house, and what you're worth. The girls that you love so much are usually the ones to set these robberies up because you trust them so much to tell them everything.

Then you got the police. You have the feds if you choose to go big time. They send confidential informants your way. They make your closest people snitch on you. They set you up for months, even years. They watch you closely. Then bam, now you're in the clink facing between three to twenty years. You lose your house, your car, your money, your family. You lose everything. You definitely lose everyone that claimed to be your friend. Your girls leave faster than your money. Everyone breaks your heart. You had all of that money and probably can barely afford to hire a lawyer. However long of a run that you had the game is now over. And quiet as kept, the ones that claim to have the most money stories be the brokest ones begging everybody for their stuff when they get to prison.

It looks like an enticing life, but 98% of the dealers that actually live that life, and for that life, end it the same way. They either die or get sent to prison. It's been shown and proven for decades. They look shiny during their run, but when it rains it pours on them. Nobody really knows because nobody really cares when they're all done and gone. Do you really want that life? It's entirely up to you if you want to become the next statistic.

Benefits of Incarceration

Coming from someone who has been incarcerated over a dozen times, I have to come out and admit that I have recognized some of the benefits of incarceration. I don't mean just benefits for myself. I mean that I've seen the benefits that others get by being incarcerated as well.

Although most of us claim to not have done anything, or want to admit we were wrong at times, our rap sheets do identify what we are really about. Robbers get robbery charges, thieves get theft charges, and murderers get murder and gun charges. It is until a person sees a pattern in their behavior that they really tend to wake up and see that this is not the life. Usually, we catch charges and bond out. We go to court. We may even get a little probation to knock out. But when these things continue to occur in your life it comes a time when you have to sit down and think clearly.

I've been to jail over a dozen times, but I've only sat down twice in all of my twelve years of going to jail. And I'm here to tell you that that is so not what's up. There has never been a better time when you should humble yourself and assess the damages that you are creating for your life.

Besides being locked in a cell, your freedom is gone. Freedom to see your family, keep your job, keep your house, open your own refrigerator. You are completely stripped. You are housed with people that are going to keep you updated about the years that they are facing. These people will be in the same cell, or pod, as you. They snore, they are messy, and smelly. They like to discuss your charges and try to scare you about the outcome. It's no good all the way around and there is nothing you can do about anything or any situation that arises outside while you are in there.

Although it can be hard to keep your sanity, they have physically locked away your body, but they can't lock up your mind. I can recall my two sit downs. I did not know when I would be released or on what conditions. I had to assess what was putting me in that situation, and why. Surely, I knew better than to blame anyone else. It most certainly had to be me. And I had plenty of time to figure it out.

I knew before I sat down that I was messing up badly. I was drinking excessively. I was numbing pains that I had in my life by turning up the bottle. Over two years my life began spiraling out of control. Now, this is my testimony. Yours is totally different, but there is an explanation for your actions and events. Surely if you don't come to a conclusion you will be back in the same predicament.

I found that I somehow at sometime took God out of my everyday life. I stopped praying. I stopped caring. I wasn't totally reckless, but I was falling short. I felt like God was sitting me down to clear my mind and allow me to recognize that I needed to slow down and give certain behaviors and habits up. I needed to definitely get back to prayer. I needed to regain control over my life. If I would have stayed on the streets I would have thought about doing these things, but then I would have turned up the bottle and dismissed the thoughts. Tomorrow would have been the same thing.

I strongly believe that God allows these situations to occur in our lives when we have lost sight of ourselves, become a danger to ourselves and society, and most importantly, when we have lost sight of His plan for our lives. We can have so much going on in the world that we fly around here on autopilot. No matter what the crime is, it is most likely a danger to someone or society. You get away with being a drunk driver, a shooter, an addict, a robber, a thief, a dealer, and more, you put yourself at risk of killing or being killed. It is good for God to step in and intervene; as most of us would be in more trouble than we could handle had we not been sat down and given a chance to have a reality check. You should do that for yourself. Be leery of the ones that constantly go to jail and don't learn a thing. But make sure that you are the one that reflects and eliminates it from your future so that your family doesn't have to suffer and you can raise your children properly. The judicial system will not hesitate to hand out years like Halloween candy for those who refuse to learn. And it only gets worse and worse the more you keep going back for similar crimes.

Looking Out for the Incarcerated

We all know someone close to us who is being imprisoned for whatever reasons. Besides those that just keep running back to prison numerous times every year, we have to look out for the incarcerated. Never forget the fact that just because they are out of sight that they don't have needs and need encouragement and love in order to survive during these difficult times that they are facing.

God allows incarceration as a way of sitting a person down to rehabilitate their minds and let them clearly see where the problem is. Situations worsen for those that don't seem to get the point. It's too easy for someone on the outside looking in to say, "it's all of their fault," or "he/she shouldn't have done that then." You have no idea what God is allowing in their life in order to get them to learn and to change something about themselves. You don't know what God may be saving them from by allowing them to be locked away right now. And although you can't do everything for a person that is incarcerated, nor would you even want to, you still should try to understand that just as sure as you need to hear 'I love you,' need support and encouragement, family contact, food, and money; someone that is incarcerated needs the same. They've just been put in a more helpless situation that is disabling them from fully providing for them self.

It should never be a problem doing what you are comfortably able to do for someone that you know would have never had a problem helping you when they were able to. To turn your back on this person is selfish and downright wrong. Once the system gets a hold on them the outcome is out of their control. Families should be able to pull together to ante up for legal defense money to assist in the fight so that their loved one doesn't get railroaded by the system; like it happens when a person has to use a public defender that works for the state to seal a conviction, thus, adding more time to a sentence to make life worse for the convicted and the family that is taking care of them while they're down. Those of us that work regularly know that twenty to thirty dollars a week is play money to us, but it will stretch out far to someone that is incarcerated. Most of us have weekly habits that exceed double that amount. You will never think about what good you can do for an out of sight person if you also put them out of mind. The emotions and the thought process of someone sitting still is much different than someone who is in motion. An inmate learns to really humble themselves and appreciate the small things.

Often times, while in the free world, a person is only focused on self, thinking, "no one would do this and that for me." Some believe already that no one loves them or cares what they're doing. People turn their backs on those convicted of drug dealing, when before, all that they did was accepted it, helped spend the fast money, and encouraged it without giving the dealer a clue that they were personally against it. What better way to show that person that you love them, care, and are sensitive about their situation than to be there to lend an ear, write a simple letter, say 'Happy Birthday,' finance whatever that you can comfortably, and just let them know that you acknowledge their existence? Coming from someone that knows that life from both ends, I know how much that it deeply means to them. If it were any problems before, I know how much they will greatly respect you and will never forget your efforts. The only ones that you can't seem to help are the idiots that don't care about life and always find a way back to jail. These people are unappreciative and must've somehow learned to fend for themselves. When Jesus can't save em, you most definitely won't.

The point is that millions of incarcerated people are doing time, but a lot of them are making the right mental changes, thinking more about their families and futures, and most are going to come home. Don't forget about them because they haven't forgotten about you. As always, what you do to help others in any situation is never overlooked by God so expect your blessings for being a blessing to someone who needed you during a difficult time that you hopefully never have to ever experience.

If it was you in that situation, you would really understand, and rewire some things the same way.

Get You Some Skills

Times have become very difficult in our society. Employment has been dwindling, crime has been on a rise, and people are struggling. What I hate the most is people seeing and hearing this and not even trying. This goes especially for the ones with felony convictions and people that don't even have any skills to begin with. I constantly find myself explaining how they need to stop complaining and get them some skills.

Ignorant thinking 101: "*Ain't no jobs out here, I'm just gonna grab me a sac to slang.*" Grabbing a sac just puts some money in your pocket and puts you at risk of prison time that is coming soon. This doesn't get you any kind of skills under your belt. When an employer wants to know what kind of skills you've had, you can't just tell him/her that you know how to empty a sac. Grown people shouldn't be so dumb.

Ignorant thinking 101: "*I got a felony, ain't nobody gonna hire me.*" There is truth to the felony thing though. A system designed to keep felons on the low end has long been a problem with finding a high paying job. Nowadays, they won't even accept your application with a felony conviction. Does that mean that you will never find a job? No. Does that mean that you will have to work harder to find a decent job? Yes. But when is it ever not a full time job to find a full time job? If you really want it and you're not just waking up one day and saying you want it and expecting it to fall into your lap, you will eventually get it.

See, more than anything, the key is that an employer wants skilled workers. They want someone with skills. I've had felony convictions for over ten years and have not missed a beat when it comes to work because I have skills. So I apply to the places that would be impressed by the amount of experience that I have. It's never failed me once. In fact, about three of these jobs never even had me fill out an application for the job. They had found someone that they could lightly train and that they didn't have to babysit. This is what gets me in the door. There is nothing worse than being 25 and 30 and have no skills at anything. Some people have very little skills because they've wasted so much time not working, doing time, or selling drugs. I wouldn't even want to hire that person with or without the felony if I was an employer. By the age of 30, you should have at least 4-8 years of experience in something. This increases your confidence and your chances of being hired. And don't expect every company to do background checks just because their ads say that they do. This especially goes for restaurants and food service places. I've been guilty of selecting NO on my apps by the 'felony conviction' section just because I used my judgment and didn't think that they would check. And sometimes I was right and sometimes I was wrong. Oh well, all they could do is not hire me, or just fire me. By the time they could fire me, I would have squeezed out a two or three day check. I'm just trying to find work, not destroy someone's company. I take pride in my work and pride in the company that I work for. These kinds of morals, when in place, will allow God to pull some strings for you and bless you. Sitting around and complaining will not move you off of the sofa though. There are people quitting and getting fired everyday from these companies. Your full time effort will put you in their place and start getting you some needed skills.

UNCLE SOULJA'S RULES FOR JOB SEARCH

1. *Want to work and be available to start now*- Really, really want it
2. *Think about where you would feel comfortable working, and apply to those places only*- Don't waste time with places that you won't even have an interest in doing that kind of work. You most likely won't get hired there anyway.
3. *Apply whether they are currently hiring or not*- Talk to someone in management. You will never know who is going to walk out or who got fired yesterday or today. You never know who is up for termination tomorrow. Don't just go off of Now Hiring ads.

The most recent applicants usually get the first chance since they are available.

4. *Look for places that match your skills-* You will get faster consideration. You will most likely like the work better and look forward to going to work every day.
5. *Have the look for the position that you are applying for-* Don't dress like a receptionist to get a restaurant job. Don't dress like a chef to get a factory job.
6. *Have knowledge of the company that you're applying to-* Ask questions and be interested in what goes on there.
7. *Show confidence that you can get the job and that you can do the job.*
8. *Pray that God understands your needs and places you right.*

Great On-The-Job Work Ethics

After working at so many different companies over the years, I have picked up some great work ethics along the way. These have subjected me to numerous advancements and praises by co-workers and managers. Some of these things I learned by doing the exact opposite. But the important thing is that I learned what to do and what not to do. Here are good ethics in no particular order.

1. *Arrive early/on time*-If you were allowed to come in when you wanted to everyone would do the same and nothing would get done on time. The work getting done on time is the main reason for being on time. Plus, you are on a schedule so if you are always late you're just playing with your own money. Managers also pay attention to the early-birds and the on-time employees. They recognize them as being prepared for the job that they are there to do. Being punctual is looked at when being considered for raises and promotions too.

2. *Positive/Good Attitude*- This is high on the list when you consider how well your day goes and somewhat how the other co-workers' day goes. A good attitude makes your day flow with ease. It keeps your temperament in control when dealing with stressful situations at work. The more you are positive and maintain a good attitude, those around you will be happier too. Positive attitudes are just as contagious as bad attitudes. Positive attitudes keep you out of altercations when dealing with others' bad attitudes.

3. *Good Attendance- Good attendance* gives employers a piece of mind that you will be there to complete the job. If you don't come in you put the company at risk of not fulfilling its

obligations correctly or on time. This puts everyone else behind and puts you at risk of losing the employer's trust. Calling in all of the time and making numerous excuses will get you fired. Good attendance will get you noticed and promoted.

4. *Honor Company Mission Statement*- When you learn what a company is all about and you understand their mission, do everything that you can to honor that mission. From the establishment of that company, a board of directors developed an objective and a way to accomplish their goals and they expect everyone to honor these objectives. It's only right that you realize that you don't own the company and don't make the rules. You just work for this company. You are obligated to do things the way that were stated to be the right way.

5. *Become the Company*- This is how managers get promoted from within. Someone sees what the company does and is about and they gave their all to be all they can be within the company. They actually cared about the quality of their work and the overall well-being of the company. They followed the mission statement and made sure everyone follows through with the plan. They love their job and care about every aspect of operation in the company.

6. *Take Pride in Your Work*- Never start a job without knowing you are going to do the very best that you can. You wouldn't want someone to cripple your company or dissatisfy your customers just because they didn't want to do the job right, for whatever reasons. Taking pride in your work shows you are a responsible worker and you will stand out. It may seem like it, but prideful work never goes unnoticed.

7. *Get Promoted*- Follow these ethics and get in where you fit it. If you desire to move up to a better position for you then make it known and apply yourself. Knowing that you plan to move up will keep you motivated to work harder than ever and it will impress more. You'll feel a great sense of accomplishment when you are promoted. You will feel even better about your job and the company that you are working for.

8. *Work diligently*- Working diligently never goes unnoticed either. It ensures that you are concerned with getting the job done. This

is a contagious quality as well. Employers love diligent employees that stand out more than the slackers.

9. *Be a Team Player*- There is usually a customer to serve in most companies, whether it be public or private. Everyone has to do their part and get along. Quality work falls apart when a team can't get alone. It is everyone's responsibility to put customers and the quality of their work first.

10. *Ask Questions*- What you don't know, never be afraid to ask. Employers respect that, and they would much rather that you ask a question before you make a mistake doing something and you don't know what you are doing.

Those that Refuse to Learn

It is awfully aggravating when you keep going through the same problems over and over again. When you have prayed and asked God to deliver you, and of course He did, but now you're right back to where you've started. You ask yourself over and over, why? You start to think that God is cursing you. You say to yourself, "I can't win for losing." You start to think that you are just supposed to stay down, come up for a little while, and fall back down. You learn to accept that in your life, so you welcome the misery.

The problem may be that you refuse to learn and follow through with the plan to keep yourself out of these troubles. A number of solutions have presented themselves to you, but you don't apply them long enough to make any kind of difference in your life. You may only be applying it enough to make the storm blow over. Then, when the wind blows the cause of the problem back to you, you blow away right with it. Taking better control and learning from the last time will keep this problem from resurfacing.

I love the example about people that go to jail. They humble themselves before the Lord in ways that they never have or would before. They acknowledge and confess their sin to Him. And they promise to never return to it. As soon as God releases them from what has been holding them down, they remain humble for a little bit, then they fall right back to what got them put away in the first place. They were able to last for a while, but wound up getting caught up again doing either the same thing or something similar. Usually, they are too ashamed to come before God again with the same problem so they learn to survive off of pure hope that He is still there for them. This hope may work in their favor and get them favorable results. But as soon as they are released they are at it again. This time they may feel like they didn't really need God like they thought they did, then they get caught up again. It just becomes a cycle.

This same cycle is true in many situations. Instead of doing what it is that we need to do; instead of doing what it is God is clearly telling us to do, we get too wrapped up in doing our own thing. This has never failed at keeping God's people caught up. When God is allowing this to happen to you and you are feeling like He is trying to teach you something about yourself, this is how you know you belong to God. It seems that evil and wicked people do and get away with whatever they want until God starts tugging at them. We will always have issues, but letting go of what is knocking us back is the answer to them not happening again.

I used to sit in jail and hear guys talk about what they were going to return to doing when they get out. I listened as they talked about how many times and how often they come to jail. It made complete sense to me. They hadn't learned a thing. Actually, they knew what it was that was holding them back. They just felt like they could be smarter the next time instead of realizing what God was showing them. They didn't realize that they weren't bigger than Him and that He was watching their every move.

The problem with refusing to learn is that you set yourself up for suicide if you don't heed to what God is telling you. You may have gotten off two or three times, but that fourth time may be the one that is going to knock you on your head. Just because you have decided not to listen you have set yourself up for disaster. A drug dealer could beat two cases, do one year on another case, and do three years on the next. That fifth case could be the one that lands him twenty or thirty years. This is all because he didn't get the point the first four times. You only get so many chances and then you're out. You have to pay attention to the signs within your own personal life. It's usually the things that we have the hardest time not doing that we need to really stop doing before it puts us down for good. You can't be so resistant to God if you are already one of His people. The last thing that you need Him to think is that you are idolizing and following your own god, or gods. He will humble you and bring you back to Him one way or another. He is being nice to you and showing you His love by giving you chances to understand and realize where you are going wrong. We are capable of realizing after the first chance. It does you no good to acknowledge God, but still be the same wicked and evil person that you've been. This kind of acknowledgment is only an attempt to make oneself feel good, and possibly an attempt to appeal to others. It is not pleasing to God. Understanding His purpose for your life is what pleases Him.

Staying Under the Radar of the Cops

Young. Black. Stereotyped. Staying under the radar of the cops is going to be one of the wisest things that you could do if you fit this description. Take it from me. I got my license at sixteen. I got my first car at seventeen. I also got my first traffic ticket at seventeen. I have probably been pulled over between thirty to forty times since, and have accumulated more than one hundred points on my driving record.

Let's just say that I wasn't the smartest driver either. I loved to race in my Monte Carlo and Cadillac. I loved to swerve on other drivers. I loved bolting up on rims and banging subwoofers. These things are what kept me in the far right lane getting questioned by 'Johnny Law.' I know now that you have to resist being an outlaw. You can't be putting other peoples' lives endanger even when you know you are a defensive driver. You have to take notice of all of the street signs and stay aware of traffic and the conditions. People can seriously be hurt if you don't. Plus, you can never be too sure where the cops are posted and/or how long they've been watching you.

The biggest problem, and costliest problem I've ever encountered is driving late at night. This is 95% of the cause of me going to jail in my lifetime. If I had avoided being on the road after three in the morning I would've definitely stayed under the radar of the cops. Drinking and driving, drugging and driving, speeding, and just being black at night in a nice car is what these cops are out here looking for at night. They know that most likely someone out that late is up to no good. And that is very true at times. If you aren't going to and from work you may not be up to anything good at that time of the night. Cops are aggressive too in the middle of the night. They snatch you out of cars, they put dogs all through your car, they harass, and they pull out guns when they get you at night. Jails are packed at night; full of drug addicts, young people, and drunks.

Not having anything to do with drugs and alcohol keeps you low key. When cops run your information they can always see your history too. Stay away from riding with drugs and being under the influence of alcohol in the car. Stay away from people with these things too. If you obey the traffic rules and stay away from being impaired you will avoid these problems. I could never understand how some people never get pulled over, when I average five or six pullovers a year. Then, I realized that these people aren't as out and about and wild as me either. I am usually illegal as soon as I put on my seatbelt; putting myself at risk all of the time. It's not cool to have to stay watching your back and driving funny when the police get behind you. This makes them aware of you. You always have something to hide. Those with nothing to hide don't worry about the cops, and don't have issues with them either. In order to save yourself from costly and annoying legal troubles, stay as far under the radar as you can from the cops. The sooner that you do, the better chances you'll have of them not causing you any problems. Your freedom and your driver's license are two things that you never want to lose in your life. Life is already hard, and can get ridiculously difficult without one or both of these.

Rap Music Influence

We all love rap music. But rap music has changed so much over the years. It is still very enjoyable, but we have to notice the turn that it is taking for the worse. With a flood of new artists dominating over the digital age and new technologies that are allowing artists the ability to reach the masses overnight, it seems that rappers are just about saying anything in every kind of way to grab attention. But they have little concern for what they are putting in the ears and the minds of the consumers.

If you pat out hamburgers for two people and put poison in one, then give the cooked burger with the poison in it to a friend, and you eat the other one; you enjoy a good meal while they get sick off of the poison. This is the same example you set when you live a straight and narrow, prosperous life, but you create music that talks of guns, drugs, sex, and violence that you no longer have anything to do with. You just put out more poison that today's society doesn't need any more of. It is put it in communities that are already falling apart by trying to imitate, dress, and live like what they hear their favorite celebrities rap about.

This music is purposely marketed this way and encouraged to be created by new and old superstars, because it sells. So much of it has dominated the minds that it sells itself like drugs do. So when you hear a rapper talking about getting rich off of 'dope' or 'crack,' don't assume that they mean the drugs. They mean the music. It sells heavily. In turn, a zoned-out society does everything the song says to do. They say everything the song says to say. They dress in everything the song says to dress in. Cliques and little groups name their groups after the existing rap group and get attention from their own sets of groupies. Big record executives see all of this idolatry and they love it. They market everything that has to do with rap music and rap lyrics to the young group of hip-hoppers who lose their whole minds to the sounds that they hear and the images that they see.

The problem can't just be blamed on rap music though. The consumer has to take responsibility for their actions; as well as the artist making the music. The consumer has to take into consideration that the lyrics that they like to hear is not suitable all of the time for kids and teens. They have to notice that kids are sitting back and quietly absorbing and silently reciting all of the words back. This is when the lyrics become poisonous. Kids have no reason to be listening to sexually explicit, violent, or dirty music. This is the responsibility of the consumer, and it can't be blamed on rap music. Music is a form of entertainment, and the artists are the entertainers. The same goes for movies and movie stars. If you would send your child out the room, or cover their eyes and ears for movies that display sexual activity or violent scenes, you should be doing the same for the music that is going into their ears.

There are many genres of music to listen to, so it's your responsibility as a consumer to choose wisely. If the music causes you to act out according to the lyrics, anything besides making you dance, you just need to grow up. People don't usually act as ignorant off of movies and video games as they tend to do with music, so something is wrong with that. Rap music has influenced broke people to buy up everything. They've become the leading consumers of fashion. The entertainers have popularized what types of cars to drive, what kinds and what size rims to ride on, which drugs to do, and which alcoholic beverages to buy. Record executives rake in the profits and tell the artists to keep up the good work. The more consumers walk around being poisoned, the more poison they will feed to others, and the more money the record companies and the artists will make. Also, the more money the liquor stores, drug dealers, clothing departments, and car lots will make. No one cares who's dying behind it, losing their families behind it, or going broke behind it. As long as the car, clothes, shoes, drugs, rims, and alcohol sales are up and keeping the economy flowing smoothly. Guess who is really out here winning?

It's hard to say that artists should be more careful with their lyrics. But why would they do that and risk losing their career when this is what society is thirsting for anyway? They are either going to profit off of it or become consumers just like us. You go to your job everyday and do things that you don't even like or want to do just to make a check. They make millions, and sometime off of one song. Ultimately, we as consumers need to control our level of influence and just enjoy the entertainment. We need to control how we're letting our children absorb messy lyrics and images. We need to distinguish what is real music and what is just pure poison that is being said by just anybody that is trying to get paid.

SOULJA SOULJA

Generation Running Wild

Structure and leadership amongst the youth and the young adults have vanished. There used to be a time where if your dad didn't raise you at least you had uncles. It now seems to be a lost generation that are guiding themselves. The new generation of youth is running wild and reckless while lacking important training that caring elders used to install in those younger than them.

When there used to be certain well known gangs in this country with established organization and leadership, there has since come this massive spinoff of the gangs that call themselves cliques. These cliques stand on much of nothing. They are just a group of youth, mostly wanna-bes, that give themselves a name and may wreck a little bit of havoc until they fade away in a few months or a few years. They have no mission, no grounds to stand on, no positive impact, few members, and no leadership. They merely have a name to call their group. They run wild trying to prove something to each other and to possibly see how big their name can become in the city. They feed off of attention only.

The problem with this generation having no guidance is that they lose respect for the older generation. This causes them to not listen to important things that the elders can show them before they bump their heads all over the place. They are raising themselves off of poisonous rap lyrics and winding up in prison at very young ages and calling that being 'real.' No one even knows what to say to this generation that 'knows it all.' The girls are just as 'bad' as the boys too.

Elders cannot just turn their backs on this wild generation, and they must continue to talk to them and positively influence them. It seems to be a

180

lot of elders that have fallen off over the years and are losing the respect of the younger generation. Now, they turn around and encourage their reckless behaviors and sit back and watch them destroy themselves; maybe with hopes that the youth will become washed up and miserable like them later on in their life.

Gangs and Cliques

The respect, the structure, and the unity of today's gangs are nothing like how they used to be. The leaders have been taken away and now everybody is running wild. Loyalty is rapidly becoming a nonexistent quality. Wanna-bes are now starting off-brand groups called 'cliques.' Gangs were originally based on doing positive things. They may have eventually spiraled out of control, but nowadays, they start out all bad. There is no leadership, no morals, and no values.

Just to show how bad society glorifies negativity, even the OG's clearly state how much damage was caused, how many people were hurt, and how they made all kinds of wrong decisions that landed them in jails and prisons. They were shot and stabbed, beaten, and had their family's tortured. But still, young people decide that this is the life that they want to live. The results are loud and clearly stated and publicized. What is this stronghold that gangs have on society?

The 70's and 80's babies have strong ties to the initiation of the gang culture. So naturally most of them, including myself, still have gang affiliation. But not many are involved in gangbanging. And just when you thought that it was over for gangbanging, now we have the initiation of cliques from the middle of the 1990's to now. Crip and Blood sets, GD and Vicelord sets still remain, but many have branched out into a bunch of clique sets as well.

Cliques are any group of people/members with a name. You don't have to do much to join most cliques, except to represent it. There is usually no initiation process and they vary from ones wanting to have the community reputation for the greatest amount of murders, drug deals, and terrorist acts to the bunch of goofies looking to be the biggest players in the city. They stand on no morals, no values, no rules, and no structure. This is why these group organizations don't quite last long at all. Their lazy structures get them mixed up with disloyal people all of the time, and soon police are able to snatch them off of the streets. Once the clique is broken down there are no more ties or affiliations so another clique will eventually spring up.

When gangs used to be about being a part of a family of people that loved one another and stuck together, now it's simply about attention seeking cliques and crews with existing rap group names. I can't wait to see the day when I see a young clique that gathers to reconstruct neighborhoods and start businesses within the city. Why aren't the cliques doing positive things in the community to show how young black males and females can invest their money wisely and not have to be crooked? Still to this day, people involved in the gangs and the cliques are losing their lives to the dumbest issues and the most obvious mistakes just to have a name. Judges are passing out years like jolly ranchers to recently added gang members that wound up on the police's hotsheet. These members are so young and so lost that they don't even know what they have coming. Imagine how much you would stand out if you were acknowledged by the community for the great contributions that you presented to society. How do you think it would feel to be looked at as a leader and a positive asset to society by the mayor and the police? I'm sure that has to be ten times better than being their enemy and constantly hiding your lifestyle from them and watching your back. Then, instead of being a part of the underworld, where the only funding seems to come from robbing, stealing, and drug money, you can be a part of the free world and have access to loans and grants and investors for real business opportunities. You can learn how it's not really as hard as you think to open a store or a service center without even using your own money.

If the gang or clique you belong to now only involves doing multiple crimes, drugs, having multiple sex partners, riding around chasing attention, and things of that nature; you aren't doing anything new.

These activities are old and played out. They don't even get any kind of respect anymore. The world is too fast paced now to even keep up with superheros and such. Nobody cares about your rap sheet, your rap lyrics, and when you make that ultimate mistake and land yourself in prison for decades it's a wrap for anything that you ever portrayed. The ones that look the dumbest are the ones that are over thirty and almost forty that mold the younger 'twenty-somethings' to have the same ignorant gangbang, sexually immoral, drug dealing mentality as they have. But these are the ones that spend every other year locked up anyway. They are too busy trying to catch up on time that they don't even realize that they can't get back. So they live through the youngsters. These aren't real OG's. Real OG's will teach you about the game and show and tell you how to do better than them. The real OG will teach you how to think more positive to avoid a lot of the traps that they and other gang members were guided right into. They won't encourage you to go out there and kill yourself. They definitely won't sit there and watch you do it.

Wonder Why They Call You Bitch

As much as I love my black women, I'd be a liar if I said that I haven't lost a little respect for them over the years. Not all, but I can't say that I've really ran into, or had any kind of relationships with a real, strong black woman. One that is well educated, has high morals and values, never been one to sleep around, doesn't have to live off of the government, treats all with respect, and a God-fearing woman. What I have grown to be very used to is much different. This also says a lot about my character, assuming that I am also just like whom I only seem to attract.

Most of the young women that claim to be so independent and respectable are the exact opposite of what they self-proclaim once you actually get to know them. Once you get passed the attractive outfits and the drunken conversation, you start to see where their fronts come in at. I strongly believe that government assistance is a great help-me-for-now for our women and children, but living off of it and not trying to do anything better to be able to come off of it is not the definition of independence. It is not the definition by far. If the assistance was taken away right now these same ladies claiming to be so independent would starve, be homeless, and helpless. Our women have got to strive to do better nowadays. It's called assistance, not dependence.

The levels of self respect have dipped to an all time low. Women refer to themselves and their friends as 'bitches' like that has ever been cute and respectable to be called a bitch. Let alone to consider yourself a bitch. They are wearing clothing that leaves nothing to the imagination except for how the sex possibly feels. It shows that they are the type of women that want doggish attention from men, and cold stares and alienation from women who respect themselves better than to present themselves in such a way. These women with lowered self respect will tell you that they don't care what anyone thinks and they do and dress as they please. They get drunk and stupid in clubs. Their friends have to carry them in the house and/or away from men that are desperate to take them and have their way with them. They look absolutely stupid and very un-lady like. Believe it or not, men that are the big bad wolves, or even the respectable men, can't stand a sloppy drunk girl. Nor would they ever respect them. They are turnoffs. They don't know what they are saying or doing. They continue to say stupid things loudly. They are passing out any and everywhere. It's ridiculous. This is why people call them 'bitch.' And it is not to be mistaken for the so-called respectable 'bitch' term that has recently taken over with the flipped-up meaning. I'm talking about the term 'bitch' that would have gotten you slapped in the face by a woman in the 80's and 90's.

Women that still sleep around with man after man, have threesomes, or engage in all sorts of sexual immoral activities thinking that nobody knows or will find out are sadly misguided and mistaken. Your name and your body, your kids and your home, your clothes and your possessions are widely discussed by men regularly in schools and homes, cars and streets, and jails and prisons all of the time and you don't even know it. Think about everything that you have said. Think about the feelings you have shared. Everything about you is discussed and passed around and even laughed at. Now you have more predators ready to push up on you and try you out. Not only that, you have to worry about your associates and family catching on to the rumors. Nothing makes a woman look more stupid, and she doesn't even have a clue that she is being passed around this way. Those that sleep around have no idea how public they are. When they do try to get in a serious relationship, people already have learned so much about them that there is no way that anyone can take them serious. They are an immediate turnoff. No matter how much a guy likes you he will never trust the 'Boys Toy.' Who wants a woman that so many men can say that they've had and can share a story about? The sexual immorality really destroys the character and the reputation of a woman. No one can ever tell them just how deep their name is in the dirt. Discussing a 'wretched' woman is grounds for big conversation amongst men and it always will be. Women tend to be like trophies to a man, and they can't resist conversing about their latest achievement.

Maybe if someone taught them more about self respect, values, and morals it wouldn't be so many women out here degrading themselves. I hate that it is glamorized so much since I do have a daughter and I despise the pressures that she will have to face. I know that I will raise her with those three important qualities with hopes that she doesn't become one of the ones acting out in these ways; and getting misused, mistreated, misled, and misguided by others. In turn, losing respect for herself and other respectable people because she didn't realize she bought that life upon herself.

Sexual Immorality amongst Men

Men have been some thirsty creatures that seek out various women to get their paws on since forever. They rarely have any regard as to what type of woman that they are actually dealing with, what kind of personality they have, or what they've done already today or yesterday. Sex is the only thing that is on their minds, and how many sexual partners they can get is the agenda. Men should be so tired of degrading themselves by now. And women should be tired of letting them.

I am not an innocent person when it comes to sexual immorality. I was also one of the ones that wake up to see who I could victimize next. I wanted to sexually involve myself with every woman that I found attractive. I wanted to have the most women, and be seen with the most women. It made me feel like the man. I felt like I was superior to those who had problems with getting girls. Chasing girls was addictive and it consumed my mind and my friends' minds. This was our way of having fun and having something to talk about.

Now that I'm older, I think about how stupid I had to be; along with every other male that participates in degrading themselves this way. It saddens me when I hear males gathered around and talking about what girl they had last night or in the past. It saddens me to hear about who their next victim is going to be. I hate to hear about who shared who. I definitely feel bad for the women who have no clue that they've become a toy, a trophy, an accomplishment to a person who cared nothing about their body, their emotions, or their privacy.

But, I also can't help the fact that I'm used to all of this too. I've been used to it since at least the fourth grade. This is how boys and men think and talk. Everyone knows that it's not a secret. It is stupid, immature, degrading, self-centered immorality. Women need to stop thinking that someone that they've met last night, tonight, or a week or two ago really cares for them like that. From a player-boy himself, that is the biggest, most beautiful lie that a woman can ever believe. And to think that women don't desire to be just as immoral as men is an even bigger lie.

Don't forget that we have a price to pay for our sins though. God is always watching. The largest, most noticeable consequence is the STD's. If a man is known to have been with lots of women, you can believe that he has contracted several STD's over time. You won't be informed about that part of his life though. A man may say that he's had something once or twice, but in all actuality he has probably been treated a dozen times. He may be carrying something now. He won't care as long as he has no symptoms, and you won't know either.

Another consequence is that the women come and go. None of them will ever stay with him. You get them fast, you lose them even faster. When he needs one to be by his side during a tough time, he will look around and see no one.

A sexually immoral man has the most trust issues. They can't trust because they deal with too many different personalities all of the time. They play and they get played. They lie and they get lied to. They disrespect and they get disrespected. What goes around comes around, but it still attacks the mind of the player. He also forgets how to be a good man to a good woman if he does happen to stumble across one. The sad part is that by the time he stumbles across a good woman he is really yearning for that love and affection. But he can't seem to get rid of the thoughts about other women, sex with other women, he has a strong need to sneak, and he never really can see himself settling down after a minute. Small imperfections that she may have will become extremely irritating and eventually he will use that as his way out. Now he can easily and comfortably go back to

SOULJA SOULJA

playing the games while he loses good woman after good woman.

God has his ways of making us pay for sexual immorality. We are already paying and don't even see it. It's way too hard to even attempt to focus on one woman if you always have your mind on several. It's nearly impossible. You definitely don't focus on God when you are focused on sex and too many women all of the time. This type of lifestyle has gone way too far and it has caused our women to disrespect us. They have no love for us and they try to mimic our behaviors now. Other women are mistreated, misused, and left hurt by our senseless and selfish acts. Instead of having several different women doing several different things to please us, we should try having one woman that we have trained to do everything that pleases us. All you have to do is let them know what it is that you like. They may not know. Then, instead of having to chase women down every day and all day, you can use some of that time and energy on something that will help you and her grow and get to the next level. I say all of this because the older that you get steady hollering about the 'bitches' and 'hoes' that you've had sex with, the dumber you look not having any of them to care about you or help you come up off of the ground-level that you are stuck on.

Ways to Kick Habits

Bad habits are not always meant to mean habits that poison our bodies or hurt ourselves or other people. Some peoples bad habits may be obsessions with doing harmless things such as; cooking, cleaning, or having bad spending habits. These types of bad habits aren't as serious as those that deal with substance abuse. There are many bad habits that require immediate attention, as they will soon have long-term effects that can and will harm individuals and those around them. They need to be noticed.

Once you acknowledge your bad habits, your next step is to find a release for it. This means finding something else that you can use to divert your attention to rather than the habit itself. If smoking is your thing, then you may want to consider buying candy instead of cigarettes. What I've noticed about bad habits is that they are a mental problem. If you can tell yourself that one thing is just as good as the other then you can will yourself into getting similar satisfaction from it. You tell yourself that you don't want any more of one and then switch to the other. Every time that you get the urge to smoke you just chew on candy instead.

Alcohol is usually a party, or a social drug. It is mostly consumed mostly when more people are indulging in it too. If you have a habit of drinking in excess when surrounded by others that are drinking nonstop, or you get the urges to overdo it by getting caught up in all of the liveliness and hype of the crowd, then you may want to slip away once you've hit your limit. You can also start filling your cup with water or juice. Use the chaser too. Just sip slow as you would if the cup was full of alcohol. Since you're already feeling social after drinking to your limit you shouldn't feel any different by sipping an alternative drink. Nobody has to know what you're drinking. You can just blend in with the rest of the crowd.

Drinking alcohol amongst a social crowd tends to make people drink more and more alcohol because the mind acknowledges that everyone has a cup and they are looking like they are really enjoying themselves, so of course you should too. Also, having something in your cup to sip, and put down, and pick back up becomes a routine action. So, you can keep something in your cup, but it doesn't have to be alcohol.

Finding a release for other habits such as excessive cursing, disrespect, and negative thinking have been difficult. But in order to break these, you have to reshape your thinking. You have to tell yourself that these things aren't what you want to no longer do. You have to explain to yourself why they aren't good for you and need to be broken. These mental issues have to be channeled by thinking about who you are affecting and how you are hurting yourself. You may be cursing too much in front of children, which may be the reason they are starting to curse. You may be disrespectful toward your mate, making them not want to talk to you or even be around you. You may find yourself having a negative opinion toward everyone who shares information with you. You may find out that people don't even seek out your advice anymore because of that. These types of bad habits have no over the counter remedy. It's all going to be about your mind restructuring, but it is possible to change these. Start by noticing that you don't really want your child, or anyone else's children to grow up with a foul mouth. You don't want your mate to walk out on you because you can't show the respect to them that they deserve, when you know that everyone deserves respect. Think about how it feels whenever you feel disrespected. Think about when you have ideas and thoughts going through your head and you feel pressed to vent to a trusted person. How would you feel if that person just instantly formed negative opinions and shot you down? Knowing the cause and the effect will help with the release.

Kicking bad habits helps us become better people. Some of us have been living with these same habits for far too long. They have made our lives and bodies worsen over the years, and have drawn people away from us. The more bad habits that we let go of, the happier we will start to see our lives becoming. The healthier we will become as well. God will be able to use us for bigger and better things that we were hindering ourselves from before by feeling like we needed something that we really didn't need.

ARE YOU CREATING TODAY'S YOU EVERYDAY?

Are you still considering the needs that it will take to become the You that you always desired to be? Do you still have the same ambition that you had when you first discovered that you have exactly what it take to become You? Is becoming You still your biggest priority?

The person with the vision and the person with the brightest ideas for how they see their individual future have a lot in common; they both realize that it is an ongoing battle and journey to make the visions or the ideas touch the surface. It is never a fly-by-night opportunity anywhere around, therefore, requiring more effort than the average visionary even knew that they possessed. The best that they could do is to continue to take action on the creation, thus, creating You.

Every day, You should be on your mind. When we let the obstacles that life are going to bring anyway get in the way, whether you are the regular you or You, we tend to deprive ourselves by allowing distractions to become excuses for why we aren't constantly moving along. We also allow these distractions to take up a larger space in our mind and our heart than the You that we should be working on daily has.

Are you Today's You, or are you Yesterday's You still? When you wake up in the morning, are you working on Today's You today? This observation can easily be determined by what is currently pressing on your mind. Most of us are still worrying and working on satisfying what has been keeping you from becoming You for most of our lives. The dreams of becoming You have been clouded by everything that gets in the way.

Ask yourself; are you Today's Jack or are you Today's Jill? It doesn't matter if you are Him or Her yet. What does matter is that every day that you rise and every night that you lie Today's You is on your mind and followed by your actions. Although we can't do it all as fast as we think it up, necessary action has to continuously take place in your mental and your physical state.

The best part of creating Today's You every day is that no one can stop you; except you. You are in complete control of how you handle yourself to be sure that you aren't mishandled. Usually, when you continue to be you, familiar distractions become a natural occurrence that will continue to hold you back from becoming You. Jack should be able to look at himself everyday and say that he is Today's Jack. If he can't, he must still be stuck in yesterday.

MOTIVATE ME FOR SUCCESS

The most appreciation comes to me in the night when most of the world is asleep. My motivation for success keeps me moving in directions that I once never seen before. My money is spent in places and in ways that others wouldn't imagine spending in. When I see others in the positions that I am striving to be in I take into consideration the struggle that they endured and the smiles that they show the world now. I use everything that I see for my future as motivation for my present.

Some days feel better than others. Some days feel slower than others. The motivation comes from knowing that everything is still moving. The motivation for success is to just keep moving. You know where you are going, so move there. Once you slow down or come to a complete stop motivation fades away. Sing your song all the way there. Pay attention to your surroundings; as some of what people say or do to you will become your biggest motivation.

Your race in your lane can be your motivation for success. A lot of leaders and successful people always knew that they would be right where they are today because they were motivated enough to know that they couldn't settle for less. It is the same with unsuccessful people. They always knew that they weren't going to fight hard, they would take the easy way out every time, and they lacked real motivation.

Sing your song because it is the music to your ears that will keep you focused on the plan ahead. Compare it to making a long drive on the highway to get to a destination. Would you say that it is a more relaxing trip with the music, or without? Song selection serves a purpose based on the way you are presently feeling and should be chosen wisely.

Even though you aren't where you want to be yet, it's about to be on. We tend to mistake our hard work and our current status with how we are being blessed and don't even recognize the blessings that are taking place in real time. Loose screws are becoming tighter, moves are being made, and time is working in our favor. Do what you have to do first to get to where you are going. God will not put you there late. You will be on time.

Use your motivation to make yourself become unrecognizable even to yourself. You will learn you faster than anyone else will. It's a good thing they don't recognize me anymore. This is the way that I know that I am making the necessary steps toward becoming Me. My motivation for success drives harmful things and people out and welcomes my future in.

PERSONAL GROWTH: TIME TO REFLECT

To achieve the level of personal growth that aligns with my purpose in life it will require a lot of time to reflect. Taking into consideration all of the rollercoaster rides, all of the pain, and all of the selfishness; I realize that I have a lot of work to do to establish the amount of personal growth that I expect to gain. To accomplish more than what I've accomplished over and over again, I will have to dedicate a lot of time to my reflection.

Paying attention to what has gotten me this far is the first part of my reflection. Everything that didn't kill me wasn't always good for me either. Or was it? It could've been that I needed those encounters to strengthen me into Today's Me. Surely, if there is some feeling of doubt about those situations there is something that needs to be changed. No need to go on attacks of my past life if it taught valuable lessons.

What have I made improvements on, and why? I reflect on this for personal growth as I discover my feelings and phases. Old feelings that don't feel good anymore show me phases that have come to pass with maturity. Some of those feelings still haunt me into today. If I don't channel these feelings I will continue to make excuses for them and slow down my personal growth.

When it's time to reflect, I ask the Lord for the insight. He enables me to stare deep into myself. Most things that won't allow my personal growth become irrelevant to my future; thus, allowing them to escape from my to-do list. People that won't allow personal growth become less important whether they are accidentally or deliberately hindering my experience. Full personal growth can't be achieved with all of the same occurrences.

To get the most out of my time to reflect, I will seclude myself from the world. Nothing else matters except the intimacy that I share with my Lord. People will throw sticks and stones and share kind or harsh words, but none will have much effect. I have to refrain from the usual teachings taught by others in order to concentrate on what I'm being taught about myself, by God. It pains me to be alone, but it strengthens me even more. I don't know how much time I'll need to reflect, but it's not a big concern to me as long as I come out of my reflection as the FULL Me.

My personal growth is important. It allows me to make better choices with my life and serve God better. What I gain when I take time to reflect shows me the love of God on a level of Him doing His part to make sure that I become Me. As long as I've been alive I've never felt so young. As long as I've felt loved I've never felt so loved. As long as I've been in motion I've never felt so ready to go.

SOULJA SOULJA

Positive People that Encourage Negativity

Often times, we confuse ourselves into thinking we are so much better than the next person when we tend to surround our self around that same person. Maybe it's the thrill of not knowing what they will do next that excites us. Some will just sit back and watch as a person destroys themselves so that we can have the last laugh, on them. The truth is that when we surround ourselves around that negativity it will wind up backfiring on us when we least expect it.

The world has always embraced negativity faster, and more than anything positive. We would much rather watch as someone continues to bump their head instead of expanding their mind. Positivity has always been recognized as square business, but negativity is embraced as in. Music that is known to be positive struggles to make it to your CD player because of a possibility that it might make you recognize yourself.

Most of us from the hood were raised around domestic abuse, substance abuse, and unstable environments that shaped our mind into embracing these situations that we know are harmful to us. These same actions were tried and tested time after time for many years, and they all shared similar results. Divorce, family separations, drug abuse, prisons, and poverty have wrecked havoc on us for years, with no end in sight. We continue to surround ourselves with negative people who have negative energy. Very few of us are willing to stand up and stop encouraging these behaviors by some of our closest people.

Just because we surround our self with people who we say we wouldn't be anything like doesn't mean that we are squeaky clean in our own self. We can't just stare at problems and not say that we aren't part of that problem. It would be hard to get a grip on the fact that you could have done something about the death of a close one, but you didn't. A lot of the time we are right there encouraging the problem without intervening and possibly creating a different outcome. You may be the most positive person, but this displays negativity.

We have a lot of people doing what they know isn't them simply to follow trends or stand out or keep from getting ridiculed. Many people have the desire and the know-how to be leaders, but it is easier to follow. New rappers that don't even have money rap about money because all of the industry stars do. You hear rap about killing others and they don't even have a gun. People follow so hard that they destroy their initial motives by trying to keep up with what they are hearing more than what they are seeing.

Even if we have done these same things mentioned, it is never too late to make a difference. If you have a partner that you know is destructive, shouldn't you TRY to keep them from destroying them self. You can't change anyone, but you can definitely encourage them to do better instead of encouraging their negative behavior.

Encourage Your Children; Don't Put Them Down

Encourage your children no matter what. Never put them down when most of what they are taught started at home in the first place. When you were little and your mother or father showed little interest in what you were so proud to show them or tell them; how did that make you feel? When you seemed to be raised by television because your parents were too busy working or too busy not paying attention; did that teach you anything valuable while transcending into adulthood? How about the bitterness that came from the separation of your parents; which in turn put you in the middle of a love-hate war that always caused you to be punished for being a product of the opposite parent?

Always encourage your children even when they always seem to be on the right track. A good reason why they could be so far ahead is because of the amount of encouragement and praise they are expecting to receive. The second that the encouragement stops, be sure that you know they will recognize it. In turn, it causes them to let go; as they tend to feel that they don't have any way to make you proud anymore.

Children recognize the rewards of simple, free encouragement from a parent; and use it to continue to make them happy. While doing so, they increase their levels and willpower and set out to achieve at all costs. Nothing can make your children happier than to know that you are happy for them and knowing that you will continue to encourage them. Studies have shown that when you don't encourage your children, they fall into all sorts of dangers including sex, drugs, gang activity, and more.

There have always been a large number of children who have appeared to be super intelligent in elementary school; into everything from honor roll, summer camps, and more. By the time they make it to high school, they are drug addicts, gang bangers, and more. A good reason is that parents were new to discovering their child's potential when they were young and quick to encourage them. By the time they were in the fifth grade, parents figured they didn't need to encourage them anymore; they'd already created a genius. They stopped encouraging.

Children will fill the void by getting encouragement from everywhere accept home. They feel let down and it is hard to get them back when they know that you don't pay attention to them. Boyfriends and girlfriends become a hot topic because they are the ones that encourage your children. Baby daddy and baby mama drama creates a barrier between parent and child, and guess who gets the worse end. Pointing out comparisons and imperfections of the opposite parent to the child creates a hostile environment that makes the child feel like a burden and unappreciated. A lot of parents channel anger for the other parent toward one or more of the children and dish out years of painful words and put downs.

In all, you should encourage your children to be all that they can be. They should never have to feel alone or unappreciated; because they didn't ask you to make them. It is every parent's responsibility to encourage your children. If not, how can you blame them for making mistakes? Don't become the one that only pays attention when trouble comes, and you have to. Regular encouragement is one of the few things that is free and goes a long way.

ABOUT THE AUTHOR

Soulja Soulja was born Rodney L. Clark Jr. in 1984. He is the creator of RapSpire Music, born in 2009. RapSpire is a positive, and inspirational brand of rap music that is designed to uplift and motivate the listeners to do better in their life and stay motivated on the purpose for their lives no matter what obstacles get in the way.

Soulja Soulja is an Indiana native that actively performs RapSpire music anywhere that he is booked. He has three children that he loves and cares for deeply. He is also the oldest child of nine children. He has three brothers and five sisters.

Soulja Soulja has been writing and recording music for eleven years to date. He has released two studio albums that are available on iTunes now, and a mixtape titled 'I Am RapSpire' that is currently available for free download. Just search 'rapspire' anywhere on the internet for more information, music downloads, and music videos.

Young: And Having Faith N The Hood is the first book title that Soulja Soulja has published to date. Other topics from Soulja Soulja have been written and will be released in early 2015, and throughout the rest of the year.

Stay tuned in for much more from Soulja Soulja and 'RapSpire Music.'